Property of Sharon Campbell

D0049594

CONVERSATIONS
A T
MIDNIGHT

HERBERT AND KAY KRAMER

CONVERSATIONS
AT
MIDNIGHT
Coming to Terms with
Dying and Death

William Morrow and Company, Inc.

NEW YORK

It is the policy of William Morrow and Company, Inc., and its imprints and affiliates, recognizing the importance of preserving what has been written, to print the books we publish on acid-free paper, and we exert our best efforts to that end.

Library of Congress Cataloging-in-Publication Data

Kramer, Herbert, 1922–1992.
    Conversations at midnight : coming to terms with dying and death / Herbert and Kay Kramer
        p.   cm.
    ISBN 0-688-12084-9
    1. Death—Psychological aspects. 2. Terminally ill—Psychology—Case studies.
I. Kramer, Kay, 1936–   .   II. Title.
BF789.D4K73   1993
155.9'37—dc20   92-19961
                                                                       CIP

Printed in the United States of America

First Edition

1 2 3 4 5 6 7 8 9 10

BOOK DESIGN BY GLEN M. EDELSTEIN

Throughout our marriage, Nancy, John, and Heidi Lazarus have joined us in the ongoing struggle, not only of coping with devastating illness, but also of confronting the ordinary events of family life where conflict of wills and feelings inevitably arise.

We have grown and learned with them in their determination to face and to resolve these as well as life's more difficult challenges with us. They have our gratitude, admiration, and respect.

We dedicate this book to them with love.

Foreword

I WAS DEEPLY TOUCHED BY THIS BOOK.

I have known Kay Kramer for many years. We first met at a workshop run by Elisabeth Kübler-Ross; shortly afterward she worked for a time at my Exceptional Cancer Patient therapy program.

In Herb and Kay's conversations, the superficial doesn't exist. The questions they share and discuss in this book are questions that each of us wants to ask and have answered. Few of us, sadly, have the courage to speak out and question as honestly. The title of the book, however, alludes directly to one possible solution. One can sense in it the darkness around us; the world is quiet. Into this darkness we present the questions; no longer can these emotions and feelings be kept sealed inside us.

Our myths and fables teach us that our path must enter the darkness of the forest if we are to find our way. To enter takes great courage. Often we are frightened, but we take heart knowing that we will ultimately lead ourselves to the goal: the precious gifts of knowledge and identity.

When one takes charcoal and compresses it, a diamond is created.

The darkness can also take our sight away. How can we

proceed when there is no light to guide us? *Conversations at Midnight* will provide you with something greater than sight: *insight*. The wisdom found in these pages will be your torch and light your path, and you need no longer fear the midnight hours.

One other sense I have of what is contained in these conversations is their power to guide us home. Just as the riderless horse finds his way back to the barn, so will this book help *you* find your own way home. Herbert and Kay's conversations will see you through life's most difficult moments.

I am sent many manuscripts and read many books. Few contain the honesty and genuineness of *Conversations at Midnight*. I know it will enrich your life, and help you bring light into its darkest corners. These conversations and this book grew out of Herb's confrontation with life-threatening cancer, but this is not a book about dying and death. It is a testament to living and life.

—DR. BERNIE SIEGEL

Acknowledgments

We acknowledge with appreciation the following people who stayed the course with us with their support and encouragement and love. They helped us to find meaning and to create beauty in a time of sadness, loss, and difficulty.

Larry Leamer, whose constant support and practical advice throughout helped us to believe that what we were writing was worth continuing.

Nancy Lazarus, who not only entered the manuscript and all its revisions into the word processor long into the night after working all day, but who also brought us kicking and screaming into the computer age by patiently and lovingly helping us to overcome our fears and trepidation about using it. Living with us this last year, she was on the front line, cheerfully lending a hand with whatever was needed. Our cook, nurse, comforter, she fed our bodies and our spirits.

Jean Lydiard, who always believed in this work and whose steadfast friendship, confidence, and love helps keep us going and whose absolute faith lifts our spirits in the darkest of times.

Charlie Mangel, who encouraged us to continue early on, and who generously and willingly offered help and gave advice whenever we needed it.

Robin MacNeil, who, when we were just about out of hope, gave us the strength to continue.

Joe and Janis Vallely, who trusted our work, worked for it, and became our friends in the process.

Patrick Walsh, M.D., who sensitively treads that fine line for a physician by knowing how to give us truth and hope at the same time, who cared about us both, and prayed for us.

Heidi Lazarus, who, in the midst of her own career struggles, devoted her energies to caring for us both every day. She took Herb to every treatment and doctor's appointment, staying with him throughout, thereby comforting him and freeing my time for working and writing. At the memorial service, she said that since she and Herb had done so many things together in his time as her father, it seemed only natural that they should do this together, too.

Elisabeth Kübler-Ross, whose example and teaching made us know that the experience of death can be full of beauty and growth as well as loss and pain.

Paul Bresnick, Mark Gompertz, and David Highfill, our editors at William Morrow and Company and Avon Books, who embraced our work with sensitivity and treated us with kindness and love.

And to all those who, everyday, give so much to people living with cancer and chronic disease. When the smallest act of kindness seems so magnified, their generous gift of love is what really helps us to live.

Contents

12   Contents

But I have lived, and have not lived in vain:
My mind may lose its force, my blood its fire,
And my frame perish even in conquering pain,
But there is that within me which shall tire
Torture and Time, and breathe when I expire . . .

Lord Byron
Childe Harold's Pilgrimage
Canto IV, Stanza 137

PROLOGUE

T HIS IS A BOOK ABOUT DEATH, about the universal, inevitable experience we share with every living thing.

Yet, despite this inevitability, in our sanitized society, we may go for many years with no personal experience of death. Our parents often live well into our own mature and even senior years. The miraculous potions and technologies of modern medicine keep what once were causes of certain death away from our door, until another day.

And when a friend or loved one is at last about to cross the borderline between life and "the undiscovered country from whose bourn no traveler returns," death comes in a hospital intensive-care unit, or in a nursing home, out of our sight or hearing.

Because death is such a stranger to us, is it any wonder that our own death seems a hostile, unnatural presence, an enemy to be held off at all costs? It is no coincidence that the despised villain of one of our most popular mythologies, the *Star Wars* trilogy, is named Darth Vader, or Death, the Invader.

To many of us, the consolations of religion, once so immediately available, have lost their power to explain death or comfort us with intimations of immortality or promises of heavenly reward.

In vain, we seek to justify the death of a child who has not even begun to experience life. In perplexity and horror, we face the sudden death in a meaningless car crash of the members of a wedding party on their way to the church. With terror, we imagine our own diagnosis of terminal illness, and we shudder at the mention of the words *cancer, heart attack*, and *AIDS*, the most devastating hit men of our era.

Yet we know, though we are afraid to admit it, that death is no stranger in our own life or in the lives of those we love. As soon as we are old enough to understand the course of human life, we realize, reluctantly, that the natural process of our growing up brings us each day closer to our winding down.

From the very moment of birth, therefore, our death is an integral part of our life. Yet we disavow it, disown it, as if it were an alien to be shunned, or, if met face to face, an enemy to be defeated.

Despite our attempts to put it aside, death is always there, standing in the shadows, asking nothing more of us than to recognize it as a part of our lives, and to claim it as our own.

When we are young and vigorous, our own death seems like a myth. As we grow older, we push death away like a friend who embarrasses us or a distasteful relative we refuse to acknowledge.

For me, as I write these words, death is a cancer moving through my skeleton and sending warning signals through my bloodstream. Within a year or two, it will claim me, but as of now, it is content simply to let me know that it is there, in my life, as it has been all along, not wanting to bother me, but waiting, like a stage-door Johnny, for the play to be over.

Since I learned of its presence, I have tried to come to terms with it, to meet it face to face, and to make it a friend instead of an adversary. This has not been easy. For the living, death is a prickly and elusive companion. But with the support and encouragement of my wife, Kay, a teacher and a therapist in death and dying, who has met death often, I have called by name the shadow that inhabits me and invited it to share, openly, the rest of my life.

When I was given the news, at age sixty-seven, that death had awakened and was stirring inside, I was afraid and saddened that I should lose the world before I was ready to let it go. The deaths of others, close to me and loved by me, had not prepared me for the news that my own ending was much nearer than I had thought. When the cancer was unmasked, I had no obvious symptoms, and so I determined that everything in my life would continue as if nothing had happened. It was to be business as usual. Full speed ahead.

But Kay refused to let this happen. She persuaded me that by failing to acknowledge the presence of death, I was, in fact, denying it. And this denial could cost me an experience rich with meaning. It could keep me closed to insights and perceptions that could greatly expand my spiritual faculties. It could answer questions about life and death that "business as usual" would reject until it was too late to receive them.

This book is to be used as needed, for information, for insight, for consolation, and for courage. Death is, after all, the vehicle that carries us from one state of being to the next, so it is well that we come to understand its workings. We are writing this book, therefore, in the hope that you, too, will find it a useful guide to a life less threatened by the death that even now, while you are thoroughly alive, is waiting to greet you and receive you and pass you on to your next stage of being.

Chapter One

EXPERIENCING DEATH

HERB'S STORY

L OOKING BACK THROUGH THE YEARS, I realize that my own knowledge of death came very early. I can still recall coming downstairs to a living room made frigid by the failure during the night of our coal-burning furnace. There, on the bottom of the cage, was my beloved canary, Peewee, lying on his back, claws in the air. I was three and inconsolable as my mother scooped up the tiny body and told me that Peewee was dead and would never sing again.

My next experience of finality was the death by asthma of my sweet, birdlike friend, Oriole. And two years after that, the drowning death of another friend, Albert, which caused not only tears and nightmares but a terrible fear of the water that lasted until, at age seven, I learned to swim.

Throughout childhood and early adolescence, death kept its distance. Then, when I was sixteen, my beloved grandmother died at the age of seventy-four, and the following year, my mother, at forty-eight, died of heart failure following minor surgery. I mourned these women, so close and dear to me, but with typical teenage self-absorption grieving soon ended, as I moved expectantly into the adventure of early adulthood.

During World War II, in India, I experienced death constantly, as each day pilot friends went out on missions from which they never returned. Beyond our remote airfield, every day was filled with the news of death on a massive, global scale. In Calcutta, during the great famine of 1943, I stepped over the bodies of starved street people, whom the rice merchants, in their lust for profits, had denied access to food. Throughout my military service I was terrified by the prospect of my own death in combat, because I wanted so desperately to return to the wife I had married just before going overseas and to the bright future I thought was mine by right.

After three years of service, I did come back. In those post-war years, the earth itself seemed to demand the replenishment of the planet, and we were only too glad to oblige. Throughout my middle twenties and thirties, creating a family of seven children and building a career, death was a stranger both to thought and experience. The years were filled with burgeoning life, with babies, with clusterings of friends, with experiencing the richness of three vital generations of family. For almost a decade, death took a holiday as we created our portion of the generation to be known as the Baby Boomers. In the midst of teeming life, even our elders seemed to defy time's blasts.

Then, in the mid 1950s, the leaves began to fall from

the family tree. Suddenly, my half brother was dead of car-
diac arrest at age forty-five, and five years later, my seventy-
year-old father collapsed as he started his morning bath, and
died of heart failure.

In 1980, my wife, whom I had met on the eve of her
sixteenth birthday and to whom I had been married for thirty-eight years, died of cancer, serene and courageous until
her last gentle breath.

Death struck over and over again. I felt orphaned,
abandoned, until I met and married Kay and added her wonderful family of three children to my own. Then, with the
final, terrible dyings of my stepmother and former mother-
in-law, both at age eighty-four, the first generation was gone.
Today, while the next generations of children and grandchildren thrive and create their own vibrant lives, death has
reaped its harvest of those I loved and lived among for more
than half a century.

But still, I savored my sweet survival and took all the
recommended measures to stave off the weaknesses of the
heart that seemed built into my genetic inheritance. I exercised, gave up meat, cut down on fats and cholesterol. And
while I guarded the front door, feeling my pulse and monitoring my blood pressure to reduce the risk of heart disease,
cancer crept in through the window and handed me the
check.

A PERSONAL ADVENTURE

The reckoning took place in the waiting room of a very
busy urologist. One week before, I had been given the news
that the biopsy of my prostate had indicated the presence of

cancer. Had it been contained? Had it spread? These were the questions to be answered in today's visit. Immediately after that initial diagnosis, I had experienced the menacing procedures of CAT scan and bone scan which would uncover the secret hiding places of the alien within.

Since it was a waiting room, we waited. And waited. For more than an hour we sat among the silent, patient patients, scanning ancient copies of *People* magazine, not daring to talk for fear of breaking some secret spell we felt had been cast over us.

Finally, we were called into the inner sanctum, a small cubicle containing three skeletal chairs and a wall full of diplomas and certificates of professional accomplishment. Again we waited until, with a sudden rush of white gown and outstretched hand, the healer appeared.

There were no niceties of greeting or small talk. "I've got the worst possible news for you," he said. Then, in a burst of professional jargon. "It's a D2, Gleason Eight, metastatic prostate cancer. Incurable but treatable. Let me repeat. There's no cure for this cancer, but it can be slowed down. We recommend a combination of a hormone, Flutamide, and an orchiectomy." He saw my quizzical look. "That's castration," he said.

And there it was. My death handed to me like a waiter's check. I looked it over and realized with surprise that I had not been staggered or dismayed at the amount of the bill. There was numbness and shock, but I felt no anger or self-pity. Nor did I for a moment think of asking the universe for an explanation, or for justice.

Instead, I accepted the verdict with a calm that surprised me. Somehow, I had been prepared for it. Because

Kay and I, in sharing her work, had talked about death so often, I was open to the news of its imminent visitation. Kay's ability to help her dying clients meet their death courageously had prepared me to accept my own.

In the two years since the sentence was pronounced, Kay and I have had many conversations concerning death. With as much objectivity as possible, I have asked the questions that have troubled me. Together, we have sought, in books and in person, the wisdom of others—physicians, clergy, poets, and philosophers. But through love and trust, I have found Kay's answers most satisfying to my skeptical mind and secular spirit. Her strong, confident, and compassionate voice is as indispensable a part of this book as it will be, some day, in the closing scenes of my life.

KAY'S STORY

It has always seemed that my work chose me, rather than I it. How did I become a therapist? Through a significant experience on the day my youngest child entered third grade. After she had left for school, I went into the kitchen and saw a dirty cereal bowl on the counter. I cried. How could anyone leave such a mess in my spotless kitchen for me to clean up? As I wept, I realized that I was crying not over the cereal bowl, but over the lack of direction of my life now that I didn't have to stay home all day in a spotless house.

It was not a unique experience for women in the early seventies. The feminist movement was in full cry. I decided

I had to change my life or suffocate. As if in answer to my unspoken thoughts, a friend appeared at my door, listened to my dilemma, and suggested I look into the chaplaincy program at Hartford Hospital. I had been active in our church's pastoral counseling groups, and I immediately felt that this might be the answer I was seeking.

Although the clinical pastoral education program was primarily for clergy, the director liked to include lay people as part of the program. And so I became a chaplain, began clinical training, and was assigned to visit individual rooms in a hospital unit.

With careful supervision, I was given more independence. I learned by examining transcripts of dialogues with patients, through discussion with supervisors and groups, and through personal therapy. Gradually, I became more comfortable talking with people who were sick or dying, and I realized I had a talent and an empathy to which the patients responded.

Then, one day, I found myself outside a closed hospital-room door. That was unusual. Most patients kept their doors open. As I stood there, I felt a strong wave of fear and foreboding about what lay behind that door. I took a breath and knocked.

A middle-aged woman came to the door and welcomed me into the room. I was scared. I wanted to run. This woman was the mother-in-law of the patient, a forty-year-old woman in the last stages of dying from stomach cancer. Her husband and her mother were in the room with Margaret, who was almost unconscious from the narcotics she was receiving. She was retching, alternately relieved and then nauseated again. Fear and horror filled my senses.

I was asked to pray. We joined hands in a circle around the bed. While saying that prayer, I realized with an intensity of feeling I had not experienced before that, beyond a doubt, beyond any concept of my belief, this was not the end of Margaret. She did not come to earth to live a short time and die a painful death. Somehow, I felt that this was my death, too. I, too, was going to die and share in this event with her. I knew also that we are all connected in some deep, basic flow. All the same. All of a piece. With her dying, something of me died. In me, a part of her would live.

When we finished the prayer, I left the room. And, while I was not certain that the fear and the sorrow in the room had lifted, I knew that I was changed, spiritually uplifted. Did it mean that life is wonderful and pain-free? No. Life is life. But I knew with certainty that some part of it continues, and that we are all inextricably connected. Our differences have no significance compared to our connections. Color, race, ethnicity, no matter: We have a divine core. A given. We are saved, and we are eternal. We are in the heart and hands of God, and the entire universe has emerged from that same spiritual core.

And that profound experience got me started.

From that time on, I was encouraged to deal with people near death. I was no longer afraid. I saw them as whole people, not broken, festering bodies. I found it easy to be with them and to understand their confusion and despair. They did not want to be abandoned and left alone out of a collective fear of death. And that is when I decided to pursue the field of social work, to become a social advocate, an educator, and a therapist at the same time.

First, though, I had to finish my undergraduate work, as I had left Syracuse University after my junior year to marry, help serve out my husband's two-year military obligation, and begin to create a succession of spotless homes in lonely places—until I realized I did not have to do that any longer.

So I got my undergraduate degree at Trinity College, at forty, the oldest graduating senior in the class, and applied to the Graduate School of Social Work at the University of Connecticut. My husband didn't have the energy or the ability to grow with me through these changes, and so we divorced, after twenty-two years of marriage, with three children on the brink of adulthood.

Some years previous to my divorce I had attended a lecture given by psychiatrist/author Elisabeth Kübler-Ross. I was so moved by her that I went up after the lecture to give her my name and address, so that I could be notified when she was ready to conduct workshops on death and dying. Soon after that she started the first Life Transitions workshop. It was a remarkable experience. I decided to dedicate myself to the work and the path that she'd been one of the first to take.

When my mother was dying of cancer, Elisabeth was lecturing in Connecticut and offered to come and speak to her. She did, and it made a tremendous difference to my mother. Elisabeth stood by her bedside and spoke the words every child wants to hear, but which my mother could not speak: "You have such a wonderful daughter. You must be very proud." I left the room and she spent an hour with my mother. My mother didn't really know who she was. She knew nothing about her work. But she did know that someone very special to me had taken the time and traveled far to be with her. When it was time for Elisabeth to leave, she told me that this was all a part of my training. I went back to my mother's room. She was very still. She said, "I feel very peaceful." I felt I had given her the most beautiful present in the world. Three weeks later, she died in peace, and I had learned from Elisabeth the most valuable lesson of all. That the events of dying and death are totally safe.

In 1979, I wrote to Elisabeth to tell her about the ending of my marriage. She suggested that I attend an upcoming workshop in Deer Isle, Maine. I used that opportunity to work through my grief and rage over my failed marriage. I found a most incredible sense of healing. Although recognizing that I still felt anger and disappointment, I no longer felt hostility, rage, and resentment toward my husband. That was a big relief; I felt released and ready to go on.

After working with people who were dying, it became clear to me that these people were really living. My task would be to help those with life-threatening diseases to look at the life instead of the disease and to learn from the threat something significant about themselves and about life.

At a workshop given by Carl Simonton and Stephanie Matthews-Simonton, pioneers in this work, I sat next to a shaven-headed surgeon from New Haven who was feeling dissatisfied with his practice and wanted to do something else. A few years later, I left my hospital job to work briefly with that doctor—Bernie Siegel, and the Exceptional Cancer Patients program—and to get on with my own career of teaching and clinical practice.

In September of 1980, I married Herb, and then, ten years later, found myself in that doctor's waiting room, when he brusquely told us that Herb was suffering incurable, meta-static prostate cancer, and that he was, within a year or two, going to die.

How did I feel when that sentence was passed? I looked at Herb, and he seemed to take the news very stoically, asking all the rational questions about treatment, prognosis, and duration. But my whole body began to shake. It seemed as if we were part of a bad movie.

I was stunned by my capacity for denial. I was sure that the outcome was not going to be serious. I had thought the doctor would say that something very simple could be done, and Herb would be fine. I was worried, but I felt overly dramatic for worrying so much, and so I denied my fear out of existence. I felt that if I could be very still and very quiet about it, it would pass us by.

Then, when we got to the doctor's office, I was totally unprepared for his opening salvo: "I've got the worst possible news. . . ." It was like a bomb going off.

I could have jumped up and run a marathon—run away from that terrible office, those terrible words. I was furious at the way he was treating us. I was angry that he was afraid to look at me, ignored me, only spoke to Herb without any regard for my feelings. I stared in disbelief. It was like a bad dream, with everything in my life changing in that one minute.

I wanted to put the whole day in reverse, as you would with a video in a VCR, to return to the waiting room and find that it was only some horrible B movie. I was shaking so that I could hardly sit still. My first impulse was to go to another doctor who would treat us with caring instead of with fear. I knew right then that we were going to fight, and I could hardly wait to get out of that office and begin to run to something I knew was better. I cried nearly nonstop for three days while Herb, as he fought off death with his own denial, cheerfully decided that whatever the second opinion, his life of work would go on as usual.

Chapter Two

WHAT IS DEATH ?

THE LIFE STORY OF EVERY HUMAN BEING is a variation on the theme of loss through death—of every pet, every friend, every loved one, until, sooner or later, the self, too, is taken. Yet this familiar companion on our journey remains a feared and hostile presence until the end; a Darth Vader, the dark assassin, who waits in shadows until he cuts us down.

Since there is no escaping death's company, doesn't it make sense to call it out of the shadows and make its acquaintance? This is the task that lies before Kay and me in the pages to come. There will be much beauty along the way. Poets and scientists, philosophers and theologians, mystics and rationalists, have all contributed over time to our knowledge of death and our ability to use this knowledge to eliminate fear and accept death's presence to enrich our lives.

But first, since we can't use it until we know what it is, let us try to answer the most fundamental question of all: What is death?

We have seen it a hundred times in movies and on television. The thin green line spikes across the medical-monitor screen with a sonarlike beep every time it hits an apogee. The patient, wired to the monitor, lies in stillness, the fitful rise and fall of his chest the only sign of continuing life. Then, the periodic beeps become one thin, unremitting whine. The peaks and valleys flatten out. Heartbeat is gone. Pulse. Breath. The brain subsides into still blankness. And that is death. The doctor wearily puts her stethoscope away. The nurse pulls the sheet over the patient's carved face. The next of kin are notified. Life gone, the grieving begins and, for those left in the land of the living, life goes on.

Breath and death. They not only are each other's perfect rhyme, they are the alpha and omega of life itself. Forget the argument over precisely when life begins in the individual. For the person projected into the world, human experience commences with that first inhalation of earth's sweet air. It ends only when the final exhalation is released and the breather no longer inhabits the shell that was his home.

The only human death I have experienced at first hand was the death of Karyl, my first wife. The surgeon who opened her abdomen quickly sealed it up again. "Three months," he said. "There's nothing more to be done." And the wasting process of a wildly metastasized stomach cancer took precisely that long to result in death. There was no pain. The anodyne of methadone and Thorazine, administered by the merciful angels of the palliative care team, saw to that. Until the moment of death, Karyl's dying was free of pain and marked by an undimmed clarity of thought and emotion.

We talked often about death—as a concept, as a looming presence—and less and less about life. In those months, as her world closed in about her, she was calm and without regrets. "It's as if I'm standing on a high plateau," she said, "looking out over past and future. There is nothing more to trouble me. I'm at peace."

While I am not enough of a psychologist to penetrate what may have been layers of denial and avoidance, I can testify to the tranquility with which she awaited the "inevitable hour."

On the morning of the day she died, I entered the hospital room to find her brushing her teeth and applying her bright-red lipstick. We spoke fitfully as she drifted in and out of sleep. At about three in the afternoon, she opened her eyes again and said, "Good-bye." "I'm not going anywhere," I said, fearful that she thought I was leaving her. "No, but I am," she said, and before I could protest, she sank into the calm slumber from which she never awoke. The gentlest sleep characterized the rest of the day. There were no cries, no labored breathing. A steady, shallow sibilance was the only sound to be heard in the darkening hospital room.

The day nurse gave way to the evening nurse. At eleven o'clock, Ann Ambrose, the night nurse who had become her dearest friend and comfort, was to come on duty. The breathing continued, steadily, unabated, until Ann entered the room. I left for a moment to walk to the elevator with my second son, who was going home to rest and change.

As I reentered the room, Ann went to the bed and took Karyl's hand, whispering, "I'm here." There was a momentary pause, the gentlest of exhalations, and the invisible border between life and death was crossed.

And I thought, *That's death? That's all there is to it? That's what terrifies us so?* And though I felt the first terrible emptiness of loss, the wound had somehow already begun to heal in the presence of that larger mystery—the easy, gentle peace of her passing.

Truly, she had "passed away." I had always hated that euphemism for the blunt, no-nonsense, Anglo-Saxon *died.* Sometime, between afternoon and nighttime, even as she continued to breathe, the essence of what was Karyl truly passed away from the racked shell of her body.

When, much later, I asked a learned physician just when she had died, he said he didn't know. Her breathing might not have been a sign of life. Her brain might have stopped functioning hours earlier. Her heart might have stopped beating long before that final exhalation. "She just passed away," he said, and that was the closest he was willing to come to a definition and a chronology of death.

Too often, in the presence of a dying person, the approach of death is never mentioned. Conversation is sanitized and the end itself, whatever it is the end of, is treated as some awful obscenity. Even friends who knew that Karyl was totally aware of her condition, filled their conversation with such empty platitudes as, "You're looking better," or "You'll lick this thing yet." They did not seem to realize that, having accepted her death and owned it, she did not want or need to be dragged back to life with empty promises. She was ready for the next adventure, the next stage in her journey. That is what she wanted to talk about and to dwell on.

It was strange to me that our doctor friends, especially, seemed incapable of dealing with the reality of Karyl's dying. It was as if her failure to be cured was an affront to their profession, the result of some moral weakness in her. This almost universal inability to come to terms with the blunt fact of her death forced her to be the comforter, to get them off the hook by demonstrating her acceptance of the presence of death.

Not morbidly or obsessively, but with the intention of becoming more familiar with this haunting, beckoning presence, we talked about our own fears of dying, our regrets for the bad times in our lives and our marriage, and our hardwon peace of mind in the face of our inevitable passing.

A philosopher by training as well as by temperament, Karyl accepted fully the view of Socrates who, as the hemlock's poison began to creep up toward his heart, was asked by a disciple if he was afraid to die. No, Socrates answered, because death offered only two possibilities: either it will be an eternal sleep, he said, or I will talk with Homer. If these options were good enough for Socrates, she said, they were good enough for her.

But of all we read and talked about in that silent hospital room, the writing that brought us the greatest comfort was a beautiful essay by Lewis Thomas in his book *Lives of a Cell.* Entitled "The Long Habit," from the seventeenth-century-writer Thomas Browne's statement "The long habit of living indisposeth us to dying," this brief discourse on death and dying links both to the natural and to the mystical the process Karyl was undergoing.

"We may be about to discover that dying is not such a bad thing to do after all," writes Thomas. "Sir William Osler took this view; he disapproved of people who spoke of the agony of death, maintaining that there was no such thing." And indeed, himself the witness to hundreds of deaths as a physician and head of one of the world's leading cancer hospitals, Thomas adds, "I have seen agony in death only once, in a patient with rabies."

The most satisfying and illuminating part of Thomas's discussion is his emphasis on the quiet efficiency of the organism's preparation for death, excepting, of course, violent death by accident or in battle. "I find myself surprised," he writes, "by the thought that dying is an all-right thing to do, but perhaps that should not surprise. It is, after all, the most ancient and fundamental of biologic functions, with its mechanisms worked out with the same attention to detail, the same provision for the advantage of the organism, the same abundance of genetic information for guidance through the stages, that we have long since become accustomed to finding in all the crucial acts of living."

Yet, even with this easy, instinctual death process, Lewis Thomas recognizes that something is missing, some assurance of permanence, some answer to the destruction of the unique self we have built by trial and error over a lifetime. "There is still that permanent vanishing of consciousness to be accounted for," he writes. "Are we to be stuck forever with this problem? Where on earth does it go? Is it simply stopped dead in its tracks, lost in humus, wasted?" No, he answers. "I prefer to think of it as somehow separated off at the filaments of its attachment and then drawn like an easy breath back into the membrane of its origin, a fresh memory for the biospherical nervous system."

As I saw with my eyes and felt, with my whole being, Karyl's last breath "drawn back into the membrane of its origin," Thomas's words came instantly to mind. "It's not a completely satisfying answer," Thomas himself admits. "I have no data on the matter." But somehow, although overly simplified, it is a concept that seems right, satisfying, plausible. If death is the end, as Socrates postulated, it is a long, dreamless sleep—Hamlet to the contrary notwithstanding. And if it is not the end, and consciousness somehow is drawn back into the "membrane of its origin," then, truly, we will talk with Homer.

Yet, even with these palatable alternatives, we are not satisfied that the answers are this unambiguous. Like everyone who has ever lived, I am concerned deeply about my dying and my death. I have questions, doubts, moments of terrible self-pity alternating with the familiar, cheerful pattern of denial. Fortunately, I can usually find answers to my gropings, my anxieties, by sharing them with Kay. And since each of my own questions has seemed to reflect the kinds of questions others might want to ask, and Kay's answers are the replies others might want to receive, these "Conversations at Midnight"—at the start of the third year of my own hard, straight look at death—constitute the heart of this book.

Chapter Three

CONVERSATIONS AT MIDNIGHT

MEDITATIONS AND CONVERSATIONS

MEDITATION 1—ON DEATH AND DYING

I lie in bed at midnight. It is now April 1991, two years since cancer was first diagnosed. During the day just past, I was told by Dr. Walsh that the pain in my hip was, indeed, caused by a further spread of the cancer. The Flutamide was not holding off all of the antigens. Without further intervention, I could count on only one year of life at most. Statistically, the average duration at this stage of metastasis was one year. Maybe I could luck out with two.

"National Institutes of Health has an experimental protocol with a drug called Suramin," Dr. Walsh told me. "I think you should try to be admitted to that protocol. It seems to be the only hope that's available, and even with Suramin, there are more unknowns than knowns. But at least it's a chance."

So I must decide: try to hold off the dying through medicine or rely on my own will and faith to see me through to the end. Even if I do gain months or even a year or more, what have I really gained, tied to an infusion pump, having to stay weeks at a time near NIH in Bethesda, risking the natural quality of my living and dying by opening myself to all manner of side effects? "Two of my patients died of the treatment," said the doctor. "But I think they've refined the protocol since then." What should I do?

It's not that I'm afraid of death. I've outlived mother and brother and am within a year of my father's passage. But the long decline is something I'm not prepared for, especially when I had been given to believe that the spread of the cancer had been checked, and I had been feeling so well.

The thought of being forced every hour of every day to be conscious of my dying, to be fitted with a catheter permanently thrust into my jugular vein, to have to attend clinic at Bethesda four or five times a week for refilling the pump, drawing blood, discussing symptoms, would all this be too much like a dying before dying, a death before death? Will it be a postponement of the suffering I fear most? Am I trying to advance against the enemy or run from the inevitable, from my appointment in Samarra?

People will say, "Herb has such courage; he's putting up such a good fight." But I'm afraid that it is really more flight than fight, an attempt to distance myself from the process of dying, which I've already begun, though as yet, I have not felt a difference, physically or emotionally.

I suppose that everyone who approaches death has the same desire to flee, to create a diversion, to put up a battle, even though the battle might be a sham. I must know more about dying. I must ask Kay.

CONVERSATION 1—ON DEATH AND DYING

HERB: It's not death I fear most, it's the suffering before dying. If, as Lewis Thomas says, death itself is so easy because of inborn genetic processes, why is the dying so often so hard?

KAY: Living, dying, and death are not divisible. The process Lewis Thomas writes about, the peace at the time of death, can be yours throughout the whole time of dying. The anguish, the fears, are not physical but psychological. They interfere with the natural process. They are not a part of it. Like prejudice or superstition, they've been learned, and they are not in harmony with natural experience. We're protected in dying by defenses that are born in us. But we need to get back in touch with them. We've lost so much of our self-awareness that we have to be reminded of what we've known all along.

H: But how about the pain, the physical suffering? How can we come to terms with that unless we are doped into insensibility? And that is certainly not natural.

K: For all the patients in whose dying I've played a part, their pain, while real, has been transcended. The worst pain is not of the body but of the mind, emotions, and spirit—the pain of loneliness, the fear of abandonment, the pain of loss, feelings of guilt or doubt—these cause the worst suffering, now that palliative care and pain control have become so effective in most cases.

I remember Sheila. Her body was being eaten away, literally, by her cancer. As you got off the elevator on her floor at the hospital, you could smell the terrible odor of rotting flesh. But her worst agony was not caused by her physical condition. It was her sense of being abandoned, being unvalued and unloved.

When I first saw her, she was almost comatose, under heavy sedation. As the sedatives were removed and her pain was controlled, I gradually won her confidence, her trust. I genuinely came to love her, and she felt cared about. While others avoided the subject of her disease and her dying, we talked about them in an open way. We were able to talk about her fears. She saw that I asked nothing of her, and that I was prepared to give her kindness and understanding. When she was able to leave the hospital, our visits continued in her home.

H: But there was still the physical decay, the loss of personal dignity to contend with. I guess I'm most afraid of the humiliation of losing physical or mental control.

K: That's why we have to face it. The body rots and decays. That is its nature. The only dignity is not in the physical but in other realms—the psychological, emotional, spiritual. There is no dignity in the body. Since when do we expect this sack of viscera to be dignified? Why is the body the target of so many rude jokes and so much embarrassment? No, we have to look to other realms. What is death with dignity? It is in the eye of the beholder. It means having control and choices and being able to act on them or to know that others are acting on our behalf. To me, personal dignity means maintaining your self-integrity, a strong sense of self-worth and value, through those terrible bodily losses.

That's why it's so important to create an environment of safety and of hope for those who are dying. You are safe here. Safe with me. Cry, curse, scream, it's all right. But reach inside yourself and try to find the natural peace and beauty that are there. Once Sheila's physical agonies were soothed, she could concentrate on the hopelessness and despair that were causing her the most pain. And, as we talked over the weeks, she relived childhood pain, lifelong disappointments, and healing began before she slipped into her final sleep, because she was able at last to accept and love herself and to forgive those by whom she felt hurt throughout her lifetime.

H: I can say very bravely now, when I have no symptoms, that, even though I've been given a very limited time to live, I don't fear death or even the prospect of a painful dying. But I do worry that I'll lose this courage, this acceptance, as death approaches.

K: Of course you feel that self-doubt now. You're still on the other side of the door, the tunnel, this dimension—whatever you call it. You have not begun to experience the transition. You have to understand that dying is a process of transition, from one state of being to another. In all the cases in which I've been involved with people who are aware of their dying, I've found a growing perception of death that the rest of us don't generally have. That is why they have so much to teach us. We learn from them. They are the experts who show us the way.

I think that's what Lewis Thomas is saying: The person who is dying develops an "other worldness," a detachment from the things of this world, even from people most loved and the things and events most to be missed. And it is not dependent on one's religious faith or whether or not you believe in a life hereafter. It is a natural part of that inborn process of leaving this state of being for another.

It clicks in at the right time. Pain subsides. The eyes of the mind turn in another direction. I've seen it so often that it's not a theory or an interpretation. We are protected in our dying by a knowledge that comes across the boundary that separates this dimension of experience from whatever comes after—the state of being that we call death.

H: Do you believe that in some way the "I," our "selfness," continues on after death?

K: Lewis Thomas says it beautifully when he writes of the conscious self being "somehow separated off at the filaments of its attachment and then drawn like an easy breath back into the membrane of its origin, a fresh memory for the biospherical nervous system." This is only one way of describing it, but it's what I believe, and what I've found brings the greatest peace and satisfaction to those who are dying. What happens in death is not the pulling of a plug, the turning of a switch, and then, eternal blackness. I'm convinced from all I've seen and studied that in death we do reconnect with the eternal force that brought us to this stage of being we now call "life." We all have an innate awareness of this connection, but the "long habit" of logic and doubt build a barrier between our limited conscious selves and the true and eternal source of our being.

H: I remember our friend Dave, who was such a skeptic about everything he considered to be "unreal." Yet, when he faced his own death, he called on you to help him to find some comfort. What was he looking for? Did you help him find it?

K: I met with Dave over a period of several weeks, at first at home and then at the hospital right up to the night he died. He sensed that he needed something but wasn't sure what it could be. A responsible, caring man, he had attended to all the practical details that would make his passing easier for his family. Now, he was curious that there might be something still unattended to that I could help him explore. What emerged was a spiritual need, a realm long unvisited in his brilliant career and responsible citizenship. At seventy-five, he was accepting, though disconsolate, about leaving his loved ones. All his life he had wanted to believe in a spiritual dimension but was unable to.

H: What did you talk about?

K: Something he didn't think he needed to talk about until suddenly it became so essential to him. And that was his spiritual nature. He really knew it all the time. We all do. But he had always thought of spiritual things apart from himself. He nourished his role as a skeptic until, when the time came, he discovered within himself another dimension, and he didn't know how to deal with it within the traditional structure.

Sometimes it takes our closeness to death to help us to put aside the things that are blocking us from the knowledge that's already within us. The knowledge that we all have a spiritual nature. But we've become so estranged from that subjective, nonrational part of ourselves that we can lose touch with it completely, if we're not brought back to it.

He needed to be able to tell someone he knew and trusted, "I'm about to die. Tell me what I need to do spiritually to come to terms with my death."

H: It's hard to believe that no-nonsense, nonbelieving Dave could ever be comfortable talking about his spiritual side. He had always dismissed it as a kind of vague mysticism.

K: But he could talk about it, because, when all the trivial concerns no longer mattered, he was able with some help to locate his spiritual self. It doesn't always happen that way. Some people are so well defended psychologically, so utterly convinced that what we know about life is all there is to know, that they just don't want to penetrate any further. An elderly man who died of cancer the very next day threw me out of his room when I merely asked if he wanted to talk about what was happening to him.

H: But Dave had always been like that. What made him change?

K: Yes, Dave had thought he was like that. His lawyer's mind was trained to deal with the "proven facts." But as the end of his life approached, he found that the things he needed to think about were things of the spirit, things he would have been embarrassed to acknowledge before.

H: How can I be certain this will happen to me?

K: Well, not everybody is a resolved success story. It's hard to stand up against easy scientific skepticism or to feel that there is some transcendent value in this throw-away age of disposable lives. But somehow Dave saw that seeking something beyond this material existence was not just wishful thinking. As we talked, he reached in and touched something in himself he had not experienced before. And that brought him great peace when the moment came for him to die. Our friend was a very beautiful person who, when I asked, generously gave permission for me to share his experience with others. What was even more generous was what he did later.

Before he died, as I usually do with my clients, I asked Dave to let me know after his passing if the things we talked about were true. I often sense that people are going to be surprised to find that death is not the end of them. Within three weeks of his death I had had two experiences that confirmed it. When I spoke to his daughter about them she said that she had had similar ones in which she sensed her father's spirit presence. It's not unusual for that to happen. The experiences involve symbols that call the person to mind, usually occur within a few weeks of death, are subjective, spontaneous, and sometimes are dismissed as coincidence, but not by people who've had them. There is a lightness and subtlety that makes it easy to miss their significance. People who are curious and trusting of their intuition and subjective experience are more apt to relate these occurrences. If one's mind is closed to them, nothing will happen, or if it does, it is missed.

I don't know of any research about this. Maybe someone will look at it as they have near-death experiences and we will be able to know more about them.

You can begin to see why this work is not as depressing as people think. There is much sadness, but the beautiful gift of sharing goes a long way to bridge the lonely gap of isolation many of us feel at one time or another. I am very grateful to Dave for what he taught me that I now have to share with others, particularly you, right now.

MEDITATION 2—ACKNOWLEDGING DEATH

Even when I was well into my twenties and thirties, I could not imagine a universe spinning on into eternity without my consciousness aboard as observer. The empty blackness of death was unimaginable and produced tremendous anxiety when I thought about it, which was as little as possible.

What a self-centered piece of egoism! As if the universe had not had a veritable infinity without me already. During the war in the Gulf, I thought of the deaths by incineration of hundreds of thousands of Iraqi soldiers and civilians, and I wondered what kind of spiritual preparation they had made for their ending. Were those who practiced religious orthodoxy better trained and prepared for death because every day of their lives they were reminded that they were part of a purposive, intentional, God-centered plan? My own skeptical attitude—half doubt, half lukewarm conviction of purpose—has made the acknowledgment of death no easier.

Because I am, despite my habits of denial, a reasonably responsible citizen, husband, and father, I have made traditional preparations for the inevitable hour. Life insurance for my wife. Pension. Will. Living will. Durable power of attorney. All are in place now. But that is only the beginning. I have shunned making decisions about burial versus cremation, funeral or memorial service, ashes scattered in the Kramer Memorial Rose Garden at Cape Cod (four rose bushes surrounding a bird bath) or placed in the earth in Kay's family plot.

Nor have I tried to inform my adult children and stepchildren of any wishes I might have about their participation in whatever ceremonies mark the occasion of my passing. Is this passivity a natural response to the unthinkable, or part of my own bewilderment in the face of the unalterable? I have been the planner and orator at other funerals of family and friends. Should I be planning now how I should be memorialized? I always used to say that I wanted my epitaph to read, "He tried." That was fine for my thirties and forties. It sounds like a pretty thin cop-out in the last year of my sixties or my early seventies, should I live that long. Everyone tries, to the level of their limitations. Is that the best I can say for myself? Or should I leave epitaph-writing to others? I can't imagine what they would say.

Karyl's ashes have long since been washed out to sea off Rhode Island. The ashes of my stepmother, Dora, have been carried down the cliffside of the Cloisters into the Hudson in the shadow of the George Washington Bridge, a place she thought one of the most beautiful. Bertha, my former mother-in-law, is beached in Rhode Island, and my father and mother and all the rest of my family lie in cemeteries miles from nowhere on Long Island or in Brooklyn.

Have I really thought seriously enough about the preparations for death during this time of dying? I must ask Kay.

CONVERSATION 2—
ACKNOWLEDGING DEATH

HERB: Why is it that so many people, even those whose profession brings them in constant contact with death and its aftermath, are so often totally unprepared when death occurs for them or for a loved one? I'm thinking of the physician who fails to get early treatment of obviously serious symptoms; the lawyer who dies without a will; the insurance executive who leaves insufficient life insurance to care for his family. Why, when death is inevitable, are so few intelligent, sensitive, otherwise mature women and men, prepared for its coming?

KAY: Our instinct for survival is so strong, so deep-seated, that we defend ourselves against death by denying it. If we bring it to the surface in conversation with friends or loved ones, we're called morbid, depressing. Talk about cemetery plots, preferences between burial and cremation, wills and last requests are hardly considered dinner-table conversation.

And when our elderly parents or grandparents try to bring our attention to fears, plans, or desires concerning their deaths, we tend to brush them off by saying, "Oh, come on, don't be so gloomy. You know you're going to outlive all of us." Or, we make a joke like, "Oh, Grandma, you're too mean to die." Or we say, "Not in front of the children, Dad. We'll talk about it later." Discussing death is a "no-no" in our culture. The American way of death is denial. Then, when it enters our lives, we try to make up for our neglect by buying the most expensive coffin, or arranging the most hurried, least-personal funeral service, just to get it behind us.

H: Do you think that this is a national characteristic or is it common to every culture—wanting to eliminate, somehow, death from life?

K: I think it's particularly American. It's part of our mythology, our sense of our youthfulness, energy, and individualism. Read Joseph Campbell's cross-cultural studies. Look at the sacred writings of the East. Other cultures are enriched by their recognition that death is central to life, not some intrusion that it's better not to think about. Death is un-American. It doesn't square with our philosophy of optimism, of progress. Even our Declaration of Independence guarantees us "Life, Liberty, and the Pursuit of Happiness." Death is the great spoiler of all three, the ants at the picnic. We know life isn't like that at all, but our science, our industry, even our religion are geared toward an affirmation of life and a rejection of the reality of death. We can see this in the strange grief reaction this country had to the Gulf War. We ignored completely, felt nothing about, the deaths of hundreds of thousands of Iraqi soldiers and civilians. Only the fact that so few of our own soldiers died counted, and even they were largely ignored in the euphoria of our "quick and painless" victory. On the other hand, we seem to be anesthetized to death real and staged on television and in movies. I've read, for example, that the average American child witnesses eight thousand real deaths and thousands more staged deaths on television before the age of sixteen.

H: But it seems to me that despite the media, we are becoming more realistic about death. There are, it seems, more books, more articles, more discussion of the subject than ever before. As our population grows older, it's becoming harder and harder to conceal the facts of death. We used to try to keep the "facts of life" from children as long as possible to preserve their innocence. Now, with a population whose fastest-growing segment is the eighty-fives and older, we have more and more people who need to face their mortality.

K: Yes, there are changes. We even have a relatively new medical specialty called geriatrics. But very few doctors are specializing in it, and very few hospitals have a department devoted specifically to the psychological or the physical needs of their aged patients. When my father was hospitalized last year, after the horrible experience of being intubated and brought back to life almost against his will, his hour-long conversation with Dr. Hamman, the geriatrician-in-chief, was the first time in his life a doctor had ever talked with him seriously, probingly, comfortingly about death and dying. It took eighty-five years for this to happen. To him, it was a great revelation. Even though he had made all the practical, financial, tax-conscious arrangements for death, he had not taken five minutes to reflect on his death and dying as the culmination of his life. I think this is a tragedy and it's happening all too often.

H: I hate to say it but there was a kind of perverse value in the fact that I had experienced my mother's death so early and had such a horrible time dealing with her funeral. I vowed, then, at seventeen, that I would not inflict that horror on any of my loved ones. And then, enlisting in the army at age nineteen, I had to think about sending allotments of money home, a will, and the basic preparations for what could be any soldier's death.

K: The army gave you an institutional support system within which to reflect on the possibility of dying while you were still young. Even though they say that no military person in harm's way thinks that he or she is going to die, every bit of military training and discipline is constructed with death in mind. You are taught not only to think about your survival, but that of your fellow soldiers. You are taught to depend on one another, and you learn that together. Because there is no experience like it in civilian life, I think you were lucky to be exposed to it so young.

H: But doctors, like soldiers, are exposed to death daily and have to reckon with it. Why, with few exceptions, are they so reluctant to prepare their patients for even the possibility of death, to be open to their feelings, their questions, their fears? When Karyl was dying, every time she wanted to talk about her death they, almost unanimously, got up and said they had other pressing business.

K: That's why it's so important that you find a doctor with whom you can communicate, if you are going to choose a strictly medical approach to your health problems. Traditionally, the medical model is to see death as a failure either of treatment on the part of the doctor or compliance on the part of the patient. We're getting more realistic about the medical model, recognizing that in many cases, it is inadequate. And doctors are trying hard to correct the arrogance of the past. They are recognizing, more and more, that health is linked not only to the body but to the mind and spirit of the patient. The abundance of anecdotal "miracle cure" books, tapes, and lectures by healers of every persuasion is proof that we are thinking about our role in our own sickness and treatment. As yet the evidence is still largely anecdotal, and most doctors, like the one who broke the news to you of your cancer, are unwilling to come from behind their white jackets and the diploma on the wall and communicate on a human level.

H: What implications does all this have for the way we should prepare ourselves for our own dying and death?

K: Well, if we are so in awe of our physician, or if he or she is so remote from us that we can't communicate, we are going to find ourselves tolerating not only incompetence, but impersonality, just at the time when we need the doctor's full attention on the human level.

H: Give me an example of what you mean.

K: The most significant one I can think of is the control of
pain. Especially in the case of cancer, a patient should become familiar with his doctor's philosophy and practice concerning pain control. As I've said, medical science right now
has reached the point where the most severe pain from cancer can be controlled, not by doping the patient into insensibility, but by blocking out the pain itself. Yet, for years,
surveys have shown that most patients experiencing severe
pain do not get enough medication even though it's available. And why? Because many doctors simply don't ask their
patients about their pain, and many patients are so in awe
of their physicians that they are hesitant to question their
orders or complain about their pain. Almost one-third of the
doctors in one recent survey don't prescribe the strongest
drugs available unless they think their patients have less than
six months to live. We still haven't come to grips with the
question of administering narcotics like marijuana or even
heroin for terminal pain. What are we afraid of? We're only
robbing pain-ridden patients of the clarity of mind and comfort of body necessary to make the transition to death as
beautiful and as peaceful as it should be. Dying is difficult
enough psychologically without adding unnecessary physical
pain to it.

H: When in the life cycle should we begin to open our children's minds to the reality of their parents' ultimate demise?
If we talk about it too early, doesn't that cause tremendous

insecurity and provoke grief long before such feelings are necessary?

K: You, yourself, have written that you were aware of death as early as three years of age. It often comes up with the death of a pet, as it did for you. I was deeply affected by my first experience with death when I was four or five years old. My brother shot a bird with a BB gun. Of course, having had cats, half-dead creatures were often deposited on our doorstep. Mom always tried to nurse them back to health, but there were the inevitable ceremonial burials. We had lots of opportunities to talk, but I learned from the way she handled those deaths, too.

All of that seems tame compared to the traumatic deaths children are being exposed to now. That's why I think it's important for parents to explore their own ideas and feelings, and to be comfortable enough talking about death so they can talk about it naturally with their children. If they don't want their children to fear death they must work to reduce their own anxieties first, so that they don't pass them on to them. Our talk about this, as with sex, should be geared to children's ability to understand.

H: I remember that when I was old enough to spend all day in synagogue during the Yom Kippur service, children were barred from that portion of the service concerned with the prayers for the dead. While I welcomed the opportunity of going outside and stretching my legs, the very fact that I was barred made death a greater mystery than it should have been. I wish now I had been able to join the Yahrzeit service and to share in the collective mourning and rejoicing that those ancient prayers express. But I never, until I was older, had the chance to share that experience with my father, and when I was older, we were already too distant to discuss the eventuality of death in our own lives. During his gradual eight-year decline because of a failing heart, we never spoke about his death, so when it came, it was a surprise to me, an incompleteness that still remains.

K: Children, even older children, tend to think of their parents as being somehow untouchable by death. They want so much to be fathered and mothered as long as possible that the idea of being orphaned is too hard to contemplate. The reality of death does not need to be terrifying. It can make us cherish all the more those whose lives are drawing to a close.

H: If we are to have the courage and the realism to acknowledge death earlier in our lives, what kind of advance preparations should we make for the ceremonials surrounding our death? Or should we leave that problem to those who will have to deal with such details after we're gone?

K: I have had clients who were so superstitious about acknowledging the reality of death by preparing for it that they were immobilized by fear and were unable to express their preferences. They seemed to think that the very acknowledgment of death would hasten its coming.

H: You mean like those couples who won't buy a layette or decorate a nursery because they are afraid that might compromise the health and safe arrival of their baby?

K: Yes. Birth and death are the great mysteries. If we have superstitious fears about them, sharing our fears and clearing the air before we begin to have babies or before our parents reach the time of their dying can be a big help.

H: As you know, Karyl was cremated, and her ashes were scattered by the children and me on a blustery, winter day on her favorite Rhode Island beach. Two months later we had a memorial service in which all of us participated. It was all very moving, but now, I think we made it harder for all of us to accept the reality of Karyl's death by not having a funeral or at least giving family and friends the chance for closure by viewing her body before cremation.

K: But weren't you honoring Karyl's wishes?

H: Yes, she wanted to spare the children the pain of seeing her cancer-ravaged body. She had expressly asked that no one view her body and that's a request I honored. We thought it would make it easier, but now I have my doubts.

K: The process of grief can be facilitated by seeing the body and realizing with our senses that the person is dead. We have a chance to see the shell of what was once a vital person and to experience with our feelings, not simply with our minds, that the body is no longer inhabited. We can fully experience the reality of the spirit being elsewhere.

H: Is it better to hold a funeral right after death than a memorial service much later?

K: People do what they can. It is a matter of custom, too. I believe that ritual for the dead that has both appropriate symbolic and literal meaning is important and can be very helpful to the grief process. As for your family, the memorial service let you work off some of your grief and express your love. But ritual immediately after death might have facilitated the grieving process by giving you all a chance to mourn realistically while feelings were raw. I watched Prince Rainier at his wife's funeral and have never forgotten it. I always thought that is how I would want my husband to look, utterly and completely grief-stricken. This seems appropriate. I think also of certain ethnic funerals in which the mourners are allowed to grieve openly, surrounded by comforters who minister to their need for support. And there are Orthodox Jews who pay mourners to bring out the grief that might otherwise be suppressed or repressed.

H: I've been opposed to the idea of an open coffin ever since I saw my mother's body, bruised and disfigured from the jouncing of the train on the long ride from Florida. But you've convinced me. I'd still like to be cremated and my ashes scattered at the Cape or buried at your gravesite. But I don't want any more denial, any more misapprehension on the part of my family about the finality of my departure. Put me in a simple, open coffin and let the truth be known. Then, let it be ashes to ashes.

K: Acknowledging death is not just something for us to do. We have to help loved ones, especially our children, acknowledge it, too. I think it can be important to have a place that is somehow blessed with the presence of one's departed loved one. You have no idea where your mother and father are buried. You've never visited their graves, have you? Yet you've told me how moving it is for you to go with me when I visit my mother's grave and my grandparents' graves in West Virginia. Having this place of memory gives a continuity and comfort in terms of family history, connectedness with the past.

Do you remember the cemetery in *Our Town*? Even though that play was a fantasy of death, it had a powerful psychological reality. The spirits hovering about the town, or resting beneath the markers on their graves, gave the town's citizens a sense of continuity. They were a constant reminder of the reality of death. Denial was impossible. Death was acknowledged. And life in *Our Town* went on. Just as it will go on in all of our homes and all our towns when each of us is called to death.

MEDITATION 3—EUTHANASIA AND SUICIDE

Last night I dreamed I lay on a high altar—not as part of a religious ceremony, not as a sacrifice, but as if I were on a high couch that had been wheeled outside from a dark room into the sun. And as I lay there, on my back, I was flooded with a radiance, a light that warmed and healed as it enveloped me. It was so real that I actually basked in it, rubbing it over my body, my ribs, my hips where the pain has struck. It was like bathing in light.

When I awoke in the darkened room, I could not dispel the reality of the experience. Somehow, I knew that it had great significance as a symbol of my true state of soul, my desire to be healed, my wanting to believe that there is, in the universe, a source of life that cares for me, that cares for everyone, that wants us well.

But then, almost immediately, the dark thoughts and fears rushed in again. What if the light is only a dream? What if there is no healing, and the corruption of my body while dying disgusts me so that I want someone to help me to bring the suffering to an end? What if the pain is so horrible, so dehumanizing, that I become something inhuman, a creature in torture, unable to experience the healing light that Kay has spoken about, that Lewis Thomas all but promises at the ending, the light of the near-death experiences?

I think of AIDS patients in the throes of their final suffering, stick thin, some covered with the purple flowers of Kaposi's sarcoma, vomiting, shaking, calling out for relief from their anguish. What kind of ending is that for a human being? And if I do cry out for someone to relieve me of the life that is in such torment, will this mean that I am trying to take the coward's way out? Will it mean that I have forestalled some natural process, some hard learning experience that I need to make the transition to the next stage of being?

I have always been opposed to the very idea of euthanasia and have been either too cowardly or too brave to entertain for an instant the thought of suicide. But that's all very fine to think and say when one is not wrapped in the barbed wire of his final suffering. I think of Dr. Jack Kevorkian, who collaborated, using his suicide machine, in the death of a woman who was entering the long, dark tunnel of Alzheimer's disease, and who then facilitated the deaths of two more people before his license was taken away. Could I ever tolerate the ministrations of such a dark angel? And what really is the difference between the withholding of nourishment, which ultimately caused the deaths of Karyl and Dora, and the active assistance in a death before its time has arrived?

What does it really mean to die with dignity? Doesn't it mean to die on an island of peace, on a bed of light, as in my dream? I must ask Kay.

CONVERSATION 3—EUTHANASIA AND SUICIDE

HERB: Two days before she died, Karyl became very tired. She wasn't in pain but seemed to be impatient that the process of dying was taking so long. And so, when the doctor made his morning rounds, she asked him, "Why don't you just put me in another room and give me something to make me die?" The doctor said, "Karyl, you know I can't do that. But I can give the order to withdraw the feeding tube and just keep you comfortable." Karyl gratefully assented, the tubes that led through her nose to her stomach were removed, and two days later she died. I just don't understand. Was this euthanasia? Was it suicide? What's the difference between what her doctor did and what that doctor with the suicide machine wants to do?

KAY: I realize that sometime there is a fine line, but to me the difference is clear. One is a natural death, hastened by the withdrawal of an artificial life-support system; the other is an active intervention in the natural process of dying. One lets unaided nature take its course; the other interferes with what could be a beautiful and important experience at the end of life. From the way you've described it, Karyl and everyone around her would have lost something precious if her death had been actively assisted. As a result, you would have felt that natural death was to be feared and avoided. Instead, you had the experience of seeing it as something peaceful and beautiful.

H: But shouldn't that decision be a private one? Why doesn't the person suffering great pain or weariness with life have the right to die when or how he chooses?

K: I think our society was right to decriminalize suicide, but right also to continue to regard assisting or abetting suicide as a criminal offense. There are so many reasons why suicide should not be made easy, and especially why participating in a suicide should not be condoned. The major reason is that suicide is irreversible. To take life, even though it is a life at the edge of death, is to commit an act that would be impermissible under any other circumstances. The Hemlock Society, for example, defends the right of people who are terminally ill to "end their own lives in a planned manner." It's as if "planning" this death somehow makes it all right. In any other circumstances, don't we call this premeditated murder, and reserve our most severe punishment for this crime? The real issue seems to me to be control. How, then, can we help people gain a sense of control short of feeling they have to take their death into their own hands?

H: True, but why doesn't the "victim" of this act, fully aware of its implications, have the right to carry it out?

K: Because simply to hasten the inevitable moment, society cannot condone the violation of the natural course of a life, the performance of an act which, if the suicide victim had lived another hour, another day, he might desperately have wanted to undo. The taking of a life is too serious; it sets too many dangerous precedents for society to allow it to happen. And it promotes fear through avoidance.

H: Are you basing your position on religious doctrine or social policy?

K: On both, I think. Speaking for myself, I believe that life is sacred; that it has a meaning; that its natural course should not be interrupted. All religions teach this sacredness, and there is something in even the least formally religious of us that knows it is true. Not to trust the process is not to trust life. I cannot live with that idea. It is inconsistent with my belief system. As public policy, actively assisted death sets dangerous, even lethal legal precedents. Since the victim's voice is stilled, who is to say that the so-called "mercy-killing" was not a coldly calculated murder? And if there is a suicide note, or a fully witnessed and notarized plan, who is to say that it was not drawn up under duress, or while the victim was emotionally or mentally incompetent?

H: In your practice, have you had to deal with terminally ill patients asking for help in dying?

K: Of course. Dying can be very hard, and the person going through it often undergoes periods of depression and extreme suffering. But from my experience, the desire for suicide is usually based on fear. And these fears can usually be resolved without recourse to ending a life who's highest moment may still lie before it. The person who feels like a burden is asking to be loved, who fears pain is asking for assurance and relief.

H: How can any fear be greater than the fear of losing one's life, even in a "planned manner"? And if that fear is overcome, shouldn't the person be allowed to go through with the voluntary taking of his life?

K: As I've said to you, the worst suffering as death approaches is not caused by physical pain, which can usually be alleviated. It's caused by depression, fear of abandonment, fear of being a burden, fear of eternal punishment, fear of the unknown. Instead of conspiring to end this suffering by ending the life, friends, relatives, physicians should be concerned with creating an environment in which fears are treated as well as physical pain. The issues creating these fears should be resolved rather than short-circuited. This is why the hospice movement is so important.

H: So you are against euthanasia under any circumstances?

K: In my experience, I've never met a patient or a family that would have been better served if the patient's death had been artificially terminated. People who support euthanasia speak of death with dignity. What is less dignified, less satisfactory than the death of a person who is unresolved and whose business with the living has not been completed? I call that the height of indignity. The dignity comes with an acceptance of the nature of existence. As I've said, the body does not have dignity.

H: But what is gained by another hour or day or week of suffering just for the sake of having a "natural" death?

K: I know you are thinking about yourself, and I appreciate that you have doubts and fears as you look ahead. What is your worst fear? Physical pain? I can promise you that there are superb therapies for assuring pain control. Even ten years ago, you saw how Karyl, suffering one of the most painful forms of cancer, was kept free of pain.

What then are you afraid of? That you will not be brave enough? That you will die alone? That your mind will be affected? I can promise you that every step will be taken to prevent any of these eventualities from taking place. Sure, there are risks. But right up until death itself, there are so many things to be learned. So much to be resolved. Knowing you, I'm sure you wouldn't want to miss any of it. Caring for the dying is a challenge full of gifts for the caregiver. Nature is impartial. It happens. We must find the salvation, redemption, and love in its most painful events.

H: And if I still wanted to die, you would still be against helping me?

K: Yes. You might as well know that now. You've already indicated in your living will and durable power of attorney that you don't want heroic measures imposed to keep you alive. No forcible intravenous. No feeding tubes. No ventilators or mechanical life supports. Everything will be done to make you physically, mentally, and emotionally comfortable because that is what the living owe to those in the process of dying. If we made euthanasia an established practice, there would be little reason to set up systems to care for and ease the pain of the dying. Quick death, administered cleanly, would be much more cost-effective than hospicelike settings in which the physical and spiritual needs of the terminally ill can be met. Once euthanasia is institutionalized, you can bet that it will be encouraged, even specified, to save money and simplify the job of the so-called health system.

H: I don't know whether your way is tougher or more merciful, more—or less—cowardly than the choice of a quick, painless exit.

K: I'll tell you what it is. It's more human. It regards the dying person with great tenderness and respect. It does not want to get him out of the way to make things easier for everyone. When I visit nursing homes and see the poor skeletons of people sitting restrained, in halls that smell of urine and of despair, I have to ask myself if it would not be more merciful to put an end to the misery of their existence. Then I remind myself that these are human beings. They are worthy of our respect and our caring. We need to make certain that they get better care, not that they get removed from our sight by removing them from our world. It is a test of our love.

H: I am sure you've read harrowing accounts of dying like Betty Rollins's *Last Wish* and Simone de Beauvoir's description of her mother's last days. In the one case, Betty Rollins helped her mother commit suicide. In the other, de Beauvoir looked on with anguish while the medical establishment made a horror show out of her mother's final days. Didn't Betty Rollins make the more humane decision?

K: I hold no brief for uncompassionate, by-the-book, arrogant doctors and hospitals. Simone de Beauvoir's mother was the victim of a too-literal interpretation of the Hippocratic oath. There was no reason her suffering should have been so prolonged by machines and artificial life supports. But in the case of Betty Rollins, in no way could I have helped my mother to commit suicide. She needed that time at the end of her life to find meaning, to express rage, to resolve conflicts, to let herself be loved by her children. To have cut that off, even if she had wanted it, would have robbed her of a time of redemption and peace. To command that a child help you to commit suicide is a final, willful expression of control. And I think that need to control shouldn't be the basis for an assisted suicide, although I have compassion for a child's trying to honor a last wish from a parent and the power of that wish. Suicide is a rage against life. If someone is bound and determined to take his or her life, that is their choice and it will happen. But we cannot condone it and must not assist it.

H: But aren't there some ultimate diseases, like Alzheimer's, where there is no possibility of redemption; where the lives of family members can be ruined with the stress and anguish of taking care of this person who is no longer, truly, a person. Where the burden is so great that many other lives can be broken? Doesn't a case like this test your beliefs to their utmost?

K: Of course. It's never easy and sometimes it's tough beyond endurance. But spiritually and philosophically, I believe euthanasia and suicide are wrong. And so we are challenged to go into places where pain and suffering are greatest, and ease the burden as best we can. Our challenge is to care for and love and nurture the life of the person who seems to be absolutely hopeless in our eyes. If we can't do much for his or her physical needs, we must, at the very least, cherish that person's spirit. We don't kill the profoundly retarded child. We don't terminate the life of the infant suffering Tay-Sachs disease, long before the inevitable process of decline into death begins. We don't because we instinctively fight to preserve the spirit which will be released when its time comes. We need this challenge to our avoidance and confusion about life on earth and what it all means.

H: This sounds pretty mystical. Isn't that same spirit released whether or not euthanasia has taken place? Why wait and prolong the suffering if it doesn't make a difference to eternity?

K: Here is where I have to rely on my personal conviction. And that is, that a soul inhabits the body. Why did it have to be this way? Who knows? For what purpose was it necessary to become manifest and materialize into what we call "life"? That's the mystery. All we know is that we've been presented with this bit of life, and I believe that the reason why we must care for those most difficult to care for, is to teach us to love, a lesson most of us need to learn over and over again, even up to the moment when we die.

Much of life seems to be very difficult and painful even for those of us who are blessed with the advantages that earth can provide. I believe that earth is a plane where this challenge of physical manifestation tests our spiritual values, ultimately helping us to return to the pure, loving source that transcends physical life and death.

MEDITATION 4—RESPONSIBILITY WITHOUT GUILT

Tomorrow, I start the five weeks of Suramin therapy at the National Cancer Institute. I have no fears about my ability to withstand the toxicity of the treatment. I am confident of my basic mental and physical health. It will be a lonely month before the one-week break that precedes another lonely month. But I am now convinced that I am doing the right thing. I must hold back the night with every weapon in the arsenal.

But I keep asking myself, "Why?" Why was I not able to help the Flutamide hold the cancer at bay? Was it my denial or my passivity that made my immune system again vulnerable to the antigen? In one of the books about self-healing, I read about a woman who had held colon cancer at bay for more than four years. She wanted to do more than sit back passively and wait for the five-year deadline to pass, so she enrolled in a program of imaging and meditation. Shortly after beginning the program, she began to feel unwell. Returning to her physician, she found that the cancer was once again spreading. When she went back to her therapist and told her what had happened, the therapist asked, "Karen, why did you want the cancer to recur?"

I found this the height of cruelty, a perfect example of the "blame the victim" syndrome that so repels me in the work of those who lead us to believe that pure will and unconditional love have the power to defeat the most insidious diseases.

But on the other hand, I wondered if there were not some truth in the therapist's remark. Had something in her life changed that made her unconsciously seek an end to the waiting, the suspense? Was she tired of harboring an invader, even one in remission? What are the boundaries between the uncontrollable onslaughts of nature, of viruses, of antigens, and the self-controllable mechanisms of resistance, of immunity, of healing?

And where, if there is a borderline over which one can cross, wittingly or unwittingly, is one's responsibility for a life-threatening illness when that line is so thoroughly concealed from the consciousness? And, of course, the real question I burn to ask is, Why was I not able to respond more forcefully to the hormone therapy, to give value to the awful orchiectomy? Had I grown weary of the fight? Had I let down my guard? Had other stresses in my life so dispirited me that, unconsciously, I longed for surcease, for someone else to share my burden—a suitable role for the National Cancer Institute?

Or was it that I did not believe sufficiently in the miracles described in endlessly worked-over anecdotes, miracles of cure produced by right thinking and feeling? I must ask Kay.

CONVERSATION 4—RESPONSIBILITY WITHOUT GUILT

HERB: I've read so many books offering sure-fire ways of preventing or self-curing cancer, and I've listened to so many tapes that promise to show *the* way that I feel like a failure because, despite everything, I was not only stricken with the most serious form of metastatic, prostate cancer, but it has continued to spread throughout my body. What did I do wrong? Can I be held responsible for my own sickness and death?

KAY: Who can answer that question? It is your question and only you have the answer, if there is one. I'm not going to second-guess your frenetic life-style, so centered on work and what you called "service" that you had little time for anything else. We've spoken about this before, over and over again, in the eleven and a half years we've been married. If stress can cause the immune system to let down so that cancer cells can grow, I suppose you've been a candidate for years, for all the years your cancer was growing secretly. The danger signs were there, but you didn't see them, or if you did, they spelled something to you besides danger. There are so many factors relating to disease and the body: genetic, metabolic, environmental, and the evidence that personality type has a role is beginning to be taken seriously. All we can do is try to keep ourselves on track as much as possible with our physical, emotional, mental, and spiritual health. Each one of these is a potential pathway to disease, so we can neglect none. It's a big job, this kind of self-awareness.

H: But a lot of the current experts say that if I have the right attitude, if I laugh a lot, if I draw pictures of my cancer and then try to erase it away, if I adopt a certain kind of diet, or if I join a self-help group, I should be able to bring about a remission, if not a cure. Most of them seem to be pointing the finger and saying that since I was responsible for the disease in the first place, I should be able to pull off its cure. Is there something just plain wrong with my attitude?

K: If an optimistic, confident attitude were all that is needed, you'd be the healthiest man in the asylum. If clean living were the key, you'd live forever. You've never smoked, never touched alcohol, you've been on a relatively fat-free diet for almost ten years. You're the original Pollyanna, running around saying, "I'm fine!" So for what can you really be held responsible?

H: But something had to be out of kilter. I don't like to think it was the hard work or the whirling dervish pace. I've always loved the pressure of my work, deadlines, meeting challenges, pleasing the most hard-to-please people. And I've felt well, particularly under stress. So what was it that did me in?

K: I don't presume to know. As your wife, I found some things that worried me. Your life program never included old age. You once told me that it was your goal to die working, being used up, spending yourself out. You made no financial plan for the latter years. It seemed as if you weren't planning on a long life. To find the answer, those of us with serious disease or those who would seek to prevent it have to ask ourselves the hard questions and willingly explore our inner life without denial. Only we have these answers, but we may have to face some hard truths to get at them.

H: So many books make it seem so easy. If you have the right attitude, love enough, listen to tapes, attend lectures, and read books, you should be able to reverse the spread of your cancer, or at least put death on hold beyond the time that medicine has given you. Doesn't this mean you are considered a failure if you do all these wonderful things and death comes upon you anyway? So, doesn't it follow that I should consider myself a failure in some area of mind or spirit because my cancer has spread, and shouldn't I feel the weight of my guilt?

K: I think you need to discover and heal your sense of failure and guilt. Everyone who works with cancer patients knows that most of those with serious involvement are going to die. Yes, there are the unexplained, "miraculous" remissions, but there are no adequate statistics to explain their cause and effect. I've had clients who meditated, changed their diets, joined groups, tried the therapy of love and laughter, changed their life-styles to relieve stress, and also followed medical protocols. And sooner or later, most of them have died. There are no fewer dead people due to cancer even with the greater awareness of these nonmedical approaches, which, by the way, I strongly advocate. There are some "miracle" cures or spontaneous remissions, delays, cessations of pain—many good things to come out of attending to oneself spiritually and emotionally as well as physically. Facing death, people can, if they are willing, find answers, not just to the specific disease that is threatening their lives, but to the many other curable, psychological, and spiritual stresses that mar their lives and inhibit their growth.

H: So you do believe that there are psychological and spiritual factors that can cause disease—my disease, for instance?

K: Of course, spiritual and emotional factors play a part in shaping our whole being. There can't be a disease in one part without there being disease in other parts, or throughout our whole system. I certainly don't understand fully the connections between all quadrants of our being. But if you want to heal yourself, you must look at the probability of disease in all parts of yourself because it is dis-ease of the spirit or the psyche that makes us vulnerable to the physical manifestations of disease in another part. Your cancer may not be cured. But in the search for the disease within you, there can be emotional and spiritual healing, and that may favorably influence your physical health. At the present state of our knowledge, we may only have an intuition that disease in the body mirrors some dis-ease in the soul, and that the site of disease has significance. The person who wants to be healed may explore this.

H: But where does this search begin? They say that almost every man over fifty is susceptible to prostate cancer. I made sure my prostate was examined digitally at every annual physical. I did not ignore symptoms. Was it my fault that a careless physician with an insensitive finger missed the call? Now that I know where and what my disease is, how should I begin to locate the center of my dis-ease? And even if I find it, isn't it too late to do much about it?

K: You have to want to know the truth of your life, apart from your illness, and then be willing to face the disease wherever it is and to explore the significance of its location. This is hard to do, especially now when you have a large enough physical battle to fight. It requires work deep in the psyche. And it certainly promises no cure. But it does promise great satisfaction and a sense of harmony within yourself and the universe. Disharmony or stress does seem to lower the resistance to disease. I have a deep respect for people who have a sense of empowerment. So, if you have a disease that threatens your life, you need to do everything that gives you a sense of control. But to say that if you eliminate stress, or learn to love better, or meditate daily, or change your diet, you'll eliminate the disease and become healthy—that's a big leap.

H: How do you present this to your clients?

K: My premise with my clients is that their disease has symbolic significance and we seek to explore this significance. As I said, this requires work deep in the psyche and deep in the past, as well. When, together, we take on that responsibility, this is what it means—examining all and everything in your life and in your being for the meaning of both your dis-ease and the particular disease that now threatens your life.

H: So here I am, minus a prostate, minus my testicles, taking hormones three times a day, involved in an experimental chemical therapy at the National Cancer Institute, eating the closest thing to a macrobiotic diet, meditating and writing my life and my death. Shouldn't the combination of these interventions demonstrate how serious I am about living instead of dying? Doesn't it mean that I'm trying to take responsibility for my fate?

K: I am very moved by your courage and your efforts. And if I had the power, I would declare you certainly worthy of cure. It's both wonderful and frustrating that you've waited for the event of metastatic disease, the whisper of death, to practice better health and self-awareness. It is never too late to do the work that furthers the growth that is possible in this life. Sometimes this is what it requires. You've certainly taken on an active role in your health and in your treatment now. It's taken a long time for you to reach this point. And you are doing what is right for you. You are covering all the bases and not giving in to hopelessness and despair. As Director of Communications for the Joseph P. Kennedy Jr. Foundation, you created the Special Olympics oath, "Let me win but if I cannot win, let me be brave in the attempt." These words spoken before every Special Olympics event all around the world are you.

I am humble in the face of this complexity about which our knowledge is so incomplete; what we know is still largely a mystery. The message to me is that it is the state of the soul that matters most. We focus on controlling those things over which we can gain control and heal those parts of ourselves that are broken, to learn the lessons life offers to teach to help us grow in life. This keeps us vital, and there is evidence that life can be extended in this manner, in the absence of fear and helplessness.

In my classes on death and dying, I talk about what Dr. Viktor Frankl, author of *Man's Search for Meaning,* identifies as a "context of meaning." We strive to create order and sense out of life's mysteries, the problem of evil and suffering. This is the task for each of us, to seek the answers to these important questions in order to make some sense of them, even if this means believing that it doesn't make sense at all.

H: I'd like to think that an early death is compensated, somehow, by a chance for continued growth in whatever realm comes after what we call life, when we pass through the door of death. But I remain a skeptic.

K: I believe that the condition of the soul is monitored and known in the mind of God, and perhaps the greatest mystery of all is its purpose, its being, and meaning. Maybe that's something we can never be aware of through our minds, our reason. And I believe this is where faith comes in. I believe the time of our birth and the time of our death are significant. Of course, there are accidents, but I believe the time of death is especially significant. We can alter it to some extent. That's what the support groups are showing. If we're in a loving, protected environment, we do seem to have the power to extend the time of our growing so that we can be better prepared when death comes.

Whenever I think about time of death, I remember a remarkable young woman named Anna, who had lived most of her adult years in hospitals and nursing homes because of a congenital heart defect. Now, at thirty-four, the options for further surgery had run out. She was determined that the remaining years of her life would be lived independently, and I had been asked to help her attain this goal. I quickly came to appreciate the sardonic sense of dark humor with which she insulated herself from the grim realities of her physical frailty. Almost from the time of birth, Anna had had every kind of experimental heart surgery possible, at a nearby leading hospital where many of the newest heart surgeries were invented and, some of them, she told me, performed on her first. She would regale me with stories. Once after a particularly complicated and long surgical procedure, she said she awoke to find a ring of physicians, white-coated and grim-faced, standing shoulder to shoulder around her bed. "Hey, you guys," she said, "am I late for my wake or something?"

Finally, she got an apartment of her own with a young graduate student as a roommate. She loved it, even though her health was failing. One day as I was preparing to visit her, I was told that she had died the day before. As I recorded her death in my progress notes, I wrote, "Anna died February 29." I stopped, and through tears and a smile, I could hear her saying, "I worked hard to live to die on this date. I know you will appreciate the joke." After this year, the anniversary of her death would disappear until four years had passed. I could see us, in the future, scratching our heads trying to figure out the number of years since her death.

A spiritualist talked to me about my mother, whom she did not know, and said that although her alcoholism seemed hopeless, her life would continue until all hope for its growth in this plane was gone. It wasn't long after that, when cancer struck and she died.

H: I can understand what happened to your mother, but how does the theory of growth, as defining the term of our life on earth, explain the death of a baby who has never had a chance to grow, or of a young soldier on the battlefield or five hundred innocent Iraqis in an air raid shelter?

K: As I said, there are accidents that bring about our own deaths and the deaths of others. There are wars and deliberate killings that frustrate the purpose of our lives. This is why war is such an affront to the universe. It's why poverty, malnutrition, and insensitivity to the needs of others are so tragic. And it's why our own abuse of our bodies through drugs, alcohol, unhealthful foods, and tobacco, is a gross example of personal irresponsibility. All of these abuses inhibit the possibilities of growth in those who are imprisoned by others or shackled by themselves to lives whose growth is obstructed. In the case of the baby born with profound physical or mental defects, or who dies soon after birth, that's where the mystery is most profound. If you grant any purpose to our existence in the universe, perhaps some souls materialize to contribute something to our growth that could not be learned in any other way. Why do saints materialize? I'm not talking about saints only in the context of Christianity, but those individuals whose very lives and deaths are messages to use to help us grow. Usually their messages are unpopular, demanding, grating, guilt-producing, and so we proceed to murder our saints, our Christs, our Lincolns, our Ghandis, our Sadats, our Martin Luther Kings, whose being here gave us such a strong image of what we might become. When their tasks were over, it really didn't matter, except to them, of course, if they lived or died. That's a hard thing to say, I know, but if you believe as I do, that there is more for us beyond this stage, then these lives and deaths do have meaning.

H: I'd like to think that my death will have meaning, to myself as well as to others. Fortunately, not being a saint, I'm in no danger of being killed except by death before I've discovered the meaning of my disease and my life.

K: The exploration is worth the effort. It may be too late for your body to respond with the strength needed to throw off your disease entirely, but your spirit, your psyche, are open to new clarity, and this will go on until you are ready to make the transition.

One of my clients had been told by her doctor that her options had run out. Nothing more could be done. She had had both breasts removed and felt herself a failure, a burden, a rotting body, even before she died. Our first goal was to eliminate her fear of death, the second to instill the conviction that while it might be too late for her body to respond, it was not too late for her soul, her capacity to love, her relationships with her husband and her children.

She determined that, in the words of the song, she was going to live until she died. She bought attractive new nightgowns designed for women who have had mastectomies. She and her husband resumed their sexual relationship. They made plans for the future. She was never deceived about her prognosis, but she was determined that she had more growing to do, both for her own sake and that of her family. Of course, she did die, but she died without fear and with new knowledge about herself and a capacity to give and receive love right up until the end.

H: I don't feel that I've stopped growing. And I realize that the only possible reason for fighting off death, as I'm doing, is to learn and to grow. The approach of death concentrates the mind on what is really important. It sharpens the senses, it gives a new perspective to one's entire history on earth. Writing this book gives us a chance to experience that process together and, I hope, to share it with others.

MEDITATION 5—UNFINISHED BUSINESS

When my stepmother, Dora, began to have delusions in her late seventies, her mother would come to visit her every morning. She would be there when Dora awoke, lying on the twin bed where my father had slept throughout the twenty years of their marriage. No matter that she had died in 1927, she was very much there, and, according to Dora, they had the kind of long, intimate conversations they never were able to have in earlier times. The visits usually ended the same way. Her mother would ask for a cup of coffee, Dora would go into the kitchen to make it, and when she returned, her mother was gone.

Her father never came. Dora missed him; she had been his favorite, while her mother had doted on her feckless brother. When Dora told the story of the latest visitation in the presence of a psychiatrist, he simply said, "You must have a lot of unfinished business with your mother." It was the first time I had heard that term used to describe a relationship that had ended badly, in misunderstanding or anger.

"Unfinished business." Thank God, I thought, I had been able to resolve most of the unfinished business between my parents and me before their deaths. Some, alas, not all. My last memory of my mother is our long good-bye at the car before I left Florida at Christmas break during my freshman year in college. Two months later she was dead. A day after the funeral, I received a letter she had written before entering the hospital entreating me to write and cheer her up. I had not written, and the guilt of my adolescent thoughtlessness has haunted me ever since. Unfinished business.

Now, as I begin my own walk through the valley of the shadow, I am acutely conscious of the need to leave no unfinished business, to pay my debts, to reconnect with old friends, to write or telephone people whom I have long neglected (or who have neglected me). Like the toothache sufferer who keeps probing the cavity with his tongue, I probe my heart for incompleteness, and I experience daily the pain of fragmented relationships with two of my children, children now in their forties, who have chosen to distance themselves from me even as they have tightened their bonds with their brothers and sisters.

My impulse, of course, is to try to fix everything before my death. If nothing else, to let them know I feel only unconditional love for them and will, if they seek it, give them my blessing and my forgiveness. And then, I think, wait a minute! I am angry and hurt. Am I picturing some Dickensian scene of resolution around my death bed, when all wounds are healed, all hurts forgiven, and everyone walks away from the body guilt-free?

How important is it, in anticipation of death, to complete all unfinished business? Is it my job to leave everyone feeling resolved and guilt-free? Did I learn more at seventeen from my mother's hurt last letter than from the inscription on her photograph, "To my son who has never disappointed me," which I knew was a lie? I must ask Kay.

CONVERSATION 5—UNFINISHED BUSINESS

HERB: I asked for time to prepare for my death, rather than blinking out unexpectedly with loose ends still untied, especially loose ends in what should be my closest relationships. Should I be more actively seeking resolution of anything that might bring pain or guilt to those I leave behind?

KAY: You so often ask "should" questions, as if there's some divine rule book presided over by a moralistic and vengeful God. "Right and wrong" is not a helpful or productive framework in which to consider these ideas.

H: But some courses of action are more helpful, less hurtful, than others. My "should" is not to God's ear but to my own heart. What is the better way to ask the question?

K: Put it in the first-person singular: "What is *my* problem with this unfinished business? What do *I* need and want to do about it?"

H: All right. I'm sure there are many people like me who feel that this lack of resolution in relationships is an impediment to healing; that the healthy connections between spirit and body are being weakened. So the first question is this: There is something in my life now that needs to be healed. Is there something I can do to heal it?

K: Yes. That is a better way to ask the question.

H: There are some relationships in my life that are not what I would like them to be. My tendency and habit are simply to say, "I forgive all," but I know that is the coward's way out. On the other hand, I don't know if I have the physical and emotional strength to attempt a deeper therapeutic resolution. Is there a middle road between blanket pardon and the too-late, in-depth attempt to work out so many tangled relationships in my family that have gone on for so many years?

K: That is such a difficult question. It would have been preferable to have had some resolution of these long-standing conflicts years ago, and some of the attempts you made were not successful. At other times, you resisted suggestions to do this.

H: I've tried to paper over the cracks and the mildew and pretend to myself and the world that "everything is fine"—my favorite words. And now I'm afraid of having waited until the last minute, when the only option left is superficial forgiveness.

K: "Blanket pardon" is what I think you mean. Forgiveness can hardly be called superficial. Forgiveness is one of the most powerful ideas in religion. Injury and forgiveness. We seem to have an innate need to make whole what is broken. Resolution is part of forgiveness, a letting go, a surrender of hurt, of anger, of grievance. But that's your work, to bring yourself to resolution, not to say all the right words, make all the right gestures, so that the death-bed scene will make everyone feel good at the moment, without really healing anything at all.

H: What about the parable of the Prodigal Son? Doesn't it teach me that, especially as a father, I should be the one to love unconditionally and forgive everything out of my greater wisdom and understanding?

K: Only if you are God, which you are not. Remember, the Prodigal Son is a parable. The father is God. It is the lesson of divine redemption that is being held out to us in the light of our terrible imperfections. It may be arrogant to think that because you are the father you have greater wisdom and understanding.

H: But I don't want to leave a lot of guilt behind, when to say, "I love you and forgive you," might make it easier for others to think of me more lovingly, to remember the closeness and not the alienation. I don't want to come back and haunt anyone as Dora's mother did sixty years later.

K: You seem concerned about how you'll be remembered—your image—rather than making things easier for someone else. I remember a phrase of Yevgeny Yevtushenko, which I find both beautiful and true: "Guilt is the teacher. Love is the lesson." At seventeen, you knew that your mother's inscription on her portrait was not truthful, and you learned from that. I think that others are able to learn more from the truth than from the blanket pardon, issued in contemplation of death. We must forgive ourselves and others, and this may make it necessary to challenge or accept the limitations by which we're bound.

H: In so many self-healing books, I've read that the way to healing is through "unconditional love." Don't you believe we're capable of that, or should try to be?

K: It's easy to talk about unconditional love or to write about it in a book. It's easy to say, "I understand all, therefore I forgive all." But I think that can be misleading. It can be a very phony, superficially comforting gesture that sometimes sounds a lot like avoidance. Try the harder work of resolving the conflict within yourself about this and turn it into something as near to truth and love as you can get. You may go amazing distances that way. That is your work, I believe, as you think about your death. Keep yourself open to resolution, but don't try to do others' work for them.

H: But for those of us who face a more immediate prospect of death, isn't there some way of speeding up the process, finding shortcuts to reconnecting broken relationships?

K: Sometimes it takes the threat of death to prompt the acute desire for resolution of conflict. We seem to have such difficulty trying to stay current with our hurts and grievances, handling them as they occur, and trying to live each day as our last. Old injuries, misunderstandings, and anger become entrenched instead of confronted and resolved. Beyond having a few words, you may not be able to work out your conflict with an individual who may be impaired or unavailable. The injured or injuring person may be dead. Their unavailability or impairment is not of your doing, and you may not have the power to heal the relationship with that person. Your work is to try to heal your own feelings. Resolution has to be sought within. This process will produce a change only in you, rather than trying to put together the broken pieces of a relationship, or worse, to sweep them under the rug of unconditional love and forgiveness when it really isn't that at all. You cannot heal another person, but you can heal your feelings about that person. Healing your feelings may then result in healing the relationship, but that comes later.

Every parent experiences parental guilt. What parents don't have regrets about their child-rearing practices? We begin the task with such joy and pure intentions, and for the most part are pleased with the beautiful people who are the result. You have been a good father. Raising and supporting seven children through the 1960s and 1970s, enabling them to go to college, graduate school, seeing them through various successes and failures, relationships, marriages, divorces, remarriages, maintaining the role of father with ex-spouses, providing for sons-in-law and grandchildren when needed. This task has been enormous, overwhelming at times. But, you've stayed the course. If it were easy, this situation would have been resolved long before now. Some business cannot be finished the way we would wish. It has to be surrendered. And that may be a truer meaning of forgiveness.

H: I have trouble acknowledging my own culpability, my own guilt in creating the distance. So many of the problems in my family have to do with my inability to recognize my role in sustaining Karyl's alcoholism, my helplessness and avoidance long after I finally did recognize what it was, and the lack of professional help at the time in understanding how to treat the problem of alcoholism. As painful as this is, I want to go into the latter stages of dying with the feeling that I have done all I can do to make this clear to everyone.

K: It's important to be accountable for your part of the problem. The great poets knew that the essence of tragedy was not in the base deed itself, but in the tragic flaw, the failure to recognize accountability until the last moment when it was too late. The inner confusion and conflict you have about these relationships need to be cleared up. Then they can be put in a perspective that is comfortable and healing. There is a lot of pain in an alcoholic family in denial. It's necessary to determine what pain is internally caused, and you are beginning to do this. It is also necessary to understand the pain that has been caused by the hostile, uncaring, or thoughtless behavior of others.

H: Absolutely, especially when I feel so strongly that so much of this hurtful behavior was unprovoked on my part. My culpability is not so much in what I have done as in my failure to deal at the time openly and honestly with the feelings I have had of hurt and confusion. But even though I recognize this failure, it still makes this time of preparation more difficult, less peaceful. Shouldn't I just reach out and try to embrace everyone again? Can't I risk that now?

K: There's the "should" again. When I hear you say you're going to put a pretty face on an unpleasant situation. I hear death, not healing. I hear despair, hopelessness, and above all, avoidance. The answer is inward, not outward. Outward is the "should." How much energy do you have right now to reach out? There are people in your life who are healing and wonderful to be with, and people who are hard to be around. How much stress do you want to take on at this time? I find it difficult to be with some people right now because I feel vulnerable to their misunderstanding, judgment, and uncaring. I feel self-protective. A secondary gain in all this is giving ourselves permission to do uncharacteristic things like telling unpleasant people that we really don't want to be with them. How do you want to live out your life? Bound by some moralistic set of "shoulds," or naturally and freely, not afraid to do and say the things you've wanted to do and say?

H: But that sounds like using the occasion of one's dying as an excuse to be selfish and vindictive, which can only create more unfinished business as death approaches. Wouldn't simple forgiveness of all of our weaknesses be most redemptive?

K: I'm not talking about selfishness. I'm talking about honesty. This is what we've learned from support groups. Health improves and life can be prolonged beyond expectation by participation in a group where people are free to express themselves openly and honestly, unbound by the "shoulds" of social convention. Statistically, such people go beyond those who are not connected to others in these positive ways. Giving ourselves permission to be more direct with others makes life less complicated. For you to batter yourself at a door that is closed would be unhealthy. Nor is it very satisfying when someone waits to be responsive to you in a positive way until you are near death and without the energy or desire to really interact with them. This intimate time is one that you may wish to spend among those who are truly able to love you without ambiguity.

H: I realize now that I've been enough of a romantic to want to create an environment of beauty and peace around me so that my death will produce no remorse, no guilt, no unfinished business in anyone's life.

K: As I think you know now this is impossible. You can't heal everything. Look at Jesus. Even with the gift of his great example and sacrifice, we are not healed on this earth.

H: I agree. So the only thing I can do now is to heal myself and those relationships that mean the most to me and have the best chance of resolution.

K: That alone is work enough. You can get practical business affairs attended to, but you cannot be responsible for being both parties to the unfinished business of relationships. You can do what you can to resolve the problem for yourself and not take on the impossible burden of being the problem solver for everyone else. This is hard because it has been a lifetime role that you have relished.

H: So there is some business that has to be left unfinished and that's just the way it is?

K: This is difficult to understand and accept. Some people are simply unavailable to do the work needed to repair their part of the relationship. And for these, all you can do is to accept the limitation and try to love the higher, spiritual essence of them. That doesn't mean you can always have an interactional relationship with them. Even at the end, they may have to keep their distance, and that's how it must be.

Let's take the case of an abused child, whose abuse the parent can't acknowledge. In terms of the relationship, there may be no resolution. So you may have to say simply, "I can't be with you right now." It is unhealthy and masochistic to keep trying to make something happen that can never be. The resolution is in accepting that this is so and making that truth livable and bearable. As I've said, it's physically and emotionally draining to pound away at a door that never opens, or if it does open, immediately slams shut again. This seems to be something we all experience at some time. We don't have to finish every piece of unfinished business except as we try to do it within ourselves. We can resolve it in our hearts and surrender it. Wish the other person, the child, the parent, the brother, the former friend well. Love their higher selves. But even in the face of death, we can't be grandiose and try to play God.

H: You know, this is the first time I've been able to say this: The greatest barrier to resolution within myself and with my family is my sense of guilt and shame over my inability to deal forthrightly and honestly with Karyl's alcoholism, and with my role in fostering and sustaining it. For years, I did not understand the nature of the sickness and certainly could not bring myself to admit that I was a part of the problem and not part of its solution. But then, when I knew more and should have been able to work with her on its resolution, I avoided my responsibility, first by escaping to Washington, and then by shutting my eyes to the hurt both of us were inflicting on ourselves and on our children. Like King David, who in his desire for Bathsheba, put her husband in harm's way, I put Karyl and my family in harm's way out of pride, ambition, and what I rationalized as my mission of service to the world. I will carry this guilt with me to the grave.

K: I hope that you will be able to forgive yourself. Then you may be able to ask forgiveness of those you have hurt, either in your heart or of them in person, and receive it. This seems closer to the resolution you have been seeking.

A Prayer: Make Me a Window

Dying, I ask *not* to be made into a stained glass window—
filled with subtleties of color and shape;

preoccupied with its own graven images—
the false stories of saints and the myths by which
we have exalted others but not praised ourselves.

Instead, let me be as transparent and as
unprofound
as a pane of clear window glass.
Let people face me, look through me,
as innocent children press against the window of
a candy store
and know the delights contained therein.

I do not ask to be free of all impurities—
bubbles, scratches, streaks.
But when these do not appear to be in the
manufacture
but through neglect or long exposure to life's
changeable weather,
let me work to erase, cleanse, and expunge these
blemishes.

Let me be a window to my own soul, too, so that
I may know with
clarity and certainty what is *my* truth as well as
the truth of others.

And when I am no longer set in place, let others
say of me—
"He let in pure light. He protected us from the
cold.
He let us see the snow and sleet and not suffer."
And, when I must be replaced, let them say,
"They don't make windows like that anymore."

MEDITATION 6—THE POWER OF HOPE

When I was about ten years old, I wrote a poem about Daniel Boone which my mother entered in a national poetry contest. It won a top award, and the poet Edwin Markham read it over the radio. Two of the lines, which have stayed with me all these years, are these:

> But through these hardships came a light,
> the radiant glow of hope,
> Which gave you the power to conquer
> the Cumberland's rocky slope.

What did I know about hope's "radiant glow"? And what do I know about hope now, almost sixty years later, as I try to sort out my feelings about this disease, its treatment, the present, and the future?

What I do know is that *hope* is a word of great ambiguity, especially now, when hope seems such a weak response to my struggle against a life-threatening illness. Should I be hoping for a cure? For a remission? For two more years of feeling well? For a relatively easy, pain-free dying? For courage? For energy to fight? For a new discovery to appear which can directly attack the prostate antigens? All of the above? And isn't hope just another form of whistling in the dark?

I suppose I entered into this experimental protocol because Dr. Walsh said there was no hope that the hormone treatment could keep the cancer in check. I suppose I subjected myself to a toxic infusion because I had no hope that I was spiritually strong enough to hope that I could reverse the disease by diet, or meditation, or will, or loving more unconditionally than I have been doing—or by any other of the New Age therapies.

I hope I have made the right decision. It seemed to have been the only one available to me because of what Kay calls my Jewish reliance on the authority of the physician. God knows, I do recognize that optimism, enthusiasm, and positive thinking are all healthy expressions of mind and will and do have an impact on the immune system and on the cancer itself. But the question arises always: How much is it healthy to hope for? How much denial is there when hope seems to fly in the face of reality?

An article in the Harvard Medical School Mental Health Letter seemed to offer some hope of a solution to my questions. It was headlined, GROUP THERAPY FOR CANCER PATIENTS: MORE HOPE. Ah, at last I might find the answer. But the article itself offered no clues. In fact, the word *hope* was never again mentioned. What it did say was that group therapy seems to be helpful for patients who have just under-gone surgery at an early stage of malignant melanoma. After group meetings for an hour and a half a week for six weeks, the therapy group, in comparison to the control, felt better, were more active, less confused, less depressed, less tired, and were coping better with the illness. Most of the therapy group, but only one third of the controls, also had increased immune-system activity.

Should I then seek safety in numbers? Find a group of my prostate-suffering peers and learn problem-solving skills and stress management? Something tells me that is not the answer for me. My hope has to come from within, and it has to be a hope that will know the way as it beckons to me. But then I think of what a little boy called "the radiant glow of hope" which gave Daniel Boone the power to conquer the Cumberland's rocky slope, and I long to find this light. I must ask Kay.

CONVERSATION 6—THE POWER OF HOPE

HERB: At this stage of the journey, I long to find the real hope, the power that will help me conquer my "Cumberland's rocky slope." But I'm afraid that I'm so well practiced in the kind of Pollyanna optimism with which I've faced my life, that what I think is hope will be just another kind of denial. I'm still searching for that "radiant glow."

KAY: But you have found that light. Your numinous experiences over the past two years have explained so much and are guiding you to new places unknown to you before. But it is particularly interesting and beautiful that you make this connection between light and hope by recalling your childhood poem. I believe you have found your ultimate hope, the kind that transcends the others on which we depend from day to day. You have been bathed and infused with a healing light, and experience the healing of the spirit.

H: How will I know that this hope is real and not just unfounded optimism?

K: Hope is not optimism. It is a state of the spirit, and the spirit has to do with our relation to the transcendent. It tests its reality. Hope is rewarded. It stands, whereas optimism is an attitude that can be contradicted by events. Optimism is vague and nonparticular. Hope is concerned with essential issues. Situations like yours challenge our thinking about the largest questions of human existence. Hope looks at all these, the limitations, the handicaps, the cruelty, and the terror and finds a light somewhere in all this darkness, the "radiant glow" you perceived as a child. Optimism is a shallower kind of blanket over things where the self is not invested. Optimism says, things are bound to get better. Hope trusts that you will be able to make them be better.

H: Are you saying that hope itself has the power to change things, to influence outcomes?

K: In all aspects of living with hope, my teachers have been my clients. One woman was hospitalized with recurrent cancer, and there were problems controlling her pain. She told me that she lived with hope. She hoped to be able to bear the next month, the next week, the next day, the next hour, all the way down to the next minute. Partializing time like that was the way she was able to keep going, to keep hope alive. I've never forgotten that brave woman. One must live with hope, and that hope may be to live through the next minute without giving up. The essential thing is that hope depends on the marshaling of your spirit energy. It's not a wish that God or fortune or the universe might come through on your behalf. Another woman with whom I worked hoped to have the strength to wash the dinner dishes after the evening meal because she wanted to make a contribution to the family that was doing so much for her.

She was able to do this until a couple of days before she died. These kinds of hopes are very modest, but as death approaches, they may define the parameters of a safe and comforting quality of life.

H: And do even these very modest hopes have the power to extend life, as the group research seems to indicate?

K: As for the relationship between hope and life extension, the evidence is there. My observation is that people seem to be able to scare themselves to death, shorten their lives by being overcome with fear. Sometimes people have so much despair that it interferes with their ability to experience hope. In therapy, we can begin with modest hopes and build from there. Hope can always be modified, enlarged, as trust takes the place of fear. It seems to operate in the context of our defenses. We are beautifully designed in this way, so that we have some built-in protection.

H: How have you experienced hope during my illness?

K: In the beginning, when you were first diagnosed as having cancer, I hoped it was not metastatic. Then I hoped you would make dramatic changes in your life that might bring about a spontaneous cure. Then I hoped we could have several healthy years of remission. Then I hoped for one year, then another. Now I hope for one more trip to our beloved alpine meadow in Switzerland where you can read aloud to me again beneath the Jungfrau. I feel this modification going on all the time. In a way, I guess it is like that brave patient. I am conscious of trying to contain my hope within a manageable amount of time. The alternative is to live in despair. One must be encouraged to find hope in the largest context in which it has the power to illuminate your life and to help you find your way. Daniel Boone wasn't simply saying, "Let me make it." He was hoping for the courage and strength to reach the next height, cross the next ravine, survive the next lightning storm, step by step, day by day, until journey's end. And that is my hope for you, to find your hope coming through the inner, spiritual journey on which you are embarking.

H: How can I tell the difference between the inner spiritual light you speak about and the wishful thinking that is so much a part of my need to make everything come out all right? All my life I've been the one who's been able to fix things for others. Now that I have lost this power, I feel very helpless in the face of the rigors of this journey. I'm not used to calling on my "spirit" for hope.

K: You are being very rational about this, and your dilemma seems to be one of trust and faith. You have had more than one spiritual experience, but now you are afraid to trust them. There were no questions in you until time had passed, and you began to do some very heavy thinking about what you were going through; and more than thinking, some very heavy feeling, which I know is not something with which you are comfortable. You have to understand that these are not experiences you have willed into creation. So what do you need to be so sure of? It is within you to decide if you are going to trust these unusual experiences and accept the spontaneous impressions you have about them.

H: Well, to be very blunt, are these experiences that seem to be putting me in touch with what you call "spirit" a part of the process of dying?

K: They are part of a process of self-discovery that is accelerated by the heightened perception of your own mortality. It has less to do with dying than with having the time and inclination to question the meaning of your life and your hope for the way you will live it out. Last year at this time, you were totally earthbound. You had no patience with any value except, perhaps, that exquisite denial you called courage. Now you are much closer to the emotional and spiritual core of your being. You are fortunate to have the time now to explore it and experience its richness. What you may want to do is to develop a discipline of meditation, morning and evening, for twenty minutes each time. Try to clear your mind of the clutter of deadlines and responsibilities. Focus on your breathing. Let your thoughts go by. See what happens. Perhaps you can meditate on the word *hope*. Concentrate on it. Let the light come to you. Don't try to intellectualize about it. Just do it and let it happen.

H: Of course, I'll try. But don't put down my hope for courage. It's a value I prize because it's so necessary in standing up to life's injustices and disappointments. Yes, I hope for the courage to climb this "Cumberland's rocky slope," which may have been a metaphor for my own life and death—perceived by me as a kind of precognition when I was a child.

K: You keep wondering if you have enough courage to get through this experience. Of course you do. You told me that you wanted your epitaph to read, "He tried." So I have no doubt about the effort you will make to be courageous in the face of death. I think the next step is critical, to concentrate on what is going to begin next. To see it as a transition, a journey to the light. You are still attached to the idea that you are lost in a dark space. It's important that you have something to hope for. You already have the critical metaphors, the radiant glow of hope, and the long journey it illuminates. So, too, the transition from this life to whatever comes after is an exciting adventure toward the light. It is a journey in which you will be protected and safe and ready to experience what comes next. I was with a patient in her last hours. She had been given quite a bit of morphine, but instead of being drugged, she expressed such a vivid sense of wonder at what was coming next, such an anticipation of the event so soon to take place, that she was almost ecstatic. This near-death experience is one I think of often. You have such a keen sense of wonder and curiosity about everything. I'm sure you will bring that to this event, too. You have lived with courage and hope your whole life, and you will not be any different as you face your own journey up Cumberland's rocky slope.

MEDITATION 7—THE GRIEF PROCESS

One of the side effects of the Suramin therapy is a misting or clouding of the eyes. It is the only annoying side effect to have been visited upon me so far in the first five weeks of the protocol.

I asked my doctor what she would suggest to clear my vision and she said, "Tears. I'll order some." Sure enough, there is a product called Tearisol and a prescription was phoned in. "It's a hell of a reversal," I said, "when a man with metastatic cancer and a guarded prognosis has to order his tears from the pharmacy."

The irony was appreciated, but the more I have thought about it, the more I realize that during my entire life, I have had a problem with tears, with grief, with rage, with any of the strong, passionate emotions that wrack our souls. As I said to my doctor, with some bemusement, "I think I can recall every moment of my life when I have cried inconsolably, just as I can recall every occasion on which I have vomited."

What a strange thing to say, I thought later. Yet, it is true, this barrier to loss of emotional control with which, from early childhood, I have protected myself from the retching, wrenching expressions of utter pain and desolation that we call grief or rage or jealousy or hate.

When my mother died, I had no tears until I received her letter from the grave asking me to write amusing letters to her while she was in the hospital for the minor operation that killed her. When my father died, I was dry-eyed until, on a plane, I read a story by William Woiwode about a long-alienated son who returns to his prairie home in North Dakota during his father's final illness and then buries his father in a coffin of his own making, calling on long-forgotten skills learned from his father when he was a child. I leaned my head against the rain-spattered window and wept silent tears. When Karyl died, I had no tears until I read aloud to Kay the October 11, 1939, entry in Karyl's diary when, on the eve of her sixteenth birthday, she came to the front door and saw, for the first time, the seventeen-year-old Herbert Kramer.

Because of this aversion to passionate, uncontrollable expression of high emotion, I have never resonated to Elisabeth Kübler-Ross's stages of grief and bereavement. I have never been able to be a part of mass grief or hysteria when tragedy strikes a public figure or the nation rejoices at the end of a war. And so, I am anesthetized against strong emotion concerning my own illness, just as I cannot conceive that my dying and my death will provoke strong feelings in those who apparently love me.

It's not that I'm undemonstrative about love. Love is an emotion I freely express in words and in actions. But I am unprepared to deal with what I know (or hope) will be the strong emotions of grief, bereavement, even anger, felt and expressed by my loved ones as my dying progresses toward the final scene. I really hope, that I, too, will be able to feel deeply when I am into the painful, wrenching part of dying and the inescapable encounter with the finality of death. How can I begin now to release those long-blocked emotions? I must ask Kay.

CONVERSATION 7—THE GRIEF PROCESS

HERB: I remember when Karyl had to be institutionalized at Hartford Hospital because she had tried to jump out of a moving automobile. It was one of the lowest, most desperate times in my life. Yet, as I was editing a speech at the office, standing next to my secretary's desk, I was totally unaware that I was whistling a pop tune. And at that moment, that desperate moment, my secretary said, "Mr. Kramer, you're the most cheerful person I have ever met." What should have been grief was the emotional blankness of denial, accompanied by a sound track of counterfeit feeling. Why have I such a difficult struggle giving myself over to the grief process? How and when does it begin? And if it can't begin, if it remains locked inside, how can there ever be understanding, acceptance, and resolution?

KAY: The grief process starts with an event, an event that, at first, seems incomprehensible, unmanageable. For you, the event is your dying. In response to the event, the grief process flows naturally and unimpeded to a resolution. That seems to be the way we are designed, like those pop-up toys you hit all the way to the floor, which then bounce right back up.

Some people get stuck or give up before the grief process has run its natural course. But left to run its course, it moves from stage to stage until there is spiritual, emotional, or intellectual resolution. Pathology is measured in terms of intensity and duration. How is the final resolution achieved?

I am drawn to Viktor Frankl's description of how some people survived the Nazi death camps while others, even though not under the direct threat of death, died. Frankl said that survival seemed to depend on being able to put the experience into a context of meaning. Those who were unresolved or who had no spiritual or intellectual framework to provide a satisfactory answer to a larger context to their lives, would invariably die. And so, people who do poorly in grief resolution are those unable to find that context of meaning, a framework that creates sense and order out of the chaos of the event that triggers the grief process. It's like the prisoner in the camp who says, "My humanity is not something to be destroyed by someone else. I am going to live long enough to get out and tell my story."

For you, I will be there to help you let the process flow to allow meaning and growth to occur. But you have to un-block your deeply entrenched denial and let this healing, natural process begin to flow.

H: I can understand getting stuck in one of the stages of the grief process that Elisabeth Kübler-Ross writes about—anger, denial, depression, shock. But to be so numbed to the event that you can do nothing but whistle and protest that "every-thing's fine" is becoming, for me, an unnatural burden, shut-ting me off from you, my loved ones, my friends who care about me and seem to feel more deeply than I do. Why should I always be the damn cheerleader?

K: Denial is one of your primary defenses, learned early and generously exercised throughout your life. It has helped you survive. I think of the traumas you experienced as a child. How frightening it must have been to struggle with your mother as she was trying to jump out of a sixteenth-story window. I was reminded of you when I saw the movie *My Life as a Dog*—the little boy having to become a clown to try to cheer up his depressed dying mother, to make her laugh. He hid his terror just as you must have.

And then there were your years of trying to deal with

Karyl's alcoholism. From all accounts, you remained cheerful throughout all sorts of embarrassing, humiliating situations. But now, there are times when you are able to reach through it. And I see it happening more right now. I was puzzled recently when you began to tell friends about the day we lay in a flower-filled meadow in Switzerland while you read *Heidi* aloud to me. You stopped speaking and put your napkin to your mouth. I wondered if you were choking on your food, as you have done before, and then was astonished to see that you were overcome with emotion, about to cry with grief. Naturally, I began to cry, which I do quite easily. I realized that this was important for you to do, but it was disturbing and heart-wrenching, because it's so out of character. Although infuriating at times, your denial spares me the pain of seeing you suffer.

H: You spoke of the incident at the Nathan-Walters's dinner table. I surprised myself with the intensity of that emotion. But I find at this stage of the journey, I am much closer to the kind of naked emotion I have so often suppressed in the past, or not felt at all. I am angry that I have been treated so shabbily by my employers; I find tears just behind, if not in my eyes, when I remember a beautiful moment we've shared, like that magic day in the meadow. I experience black despair at the knowledge that this treatment, my last hope for more time, did not work, and I am going to be left weakened, compromised, vulnerable, an old, sick man on a cane. This seems an outrageous injustice. But then, I feel the old terror that strong emotion means loss of control, and I set out deliberately to tamp it down. I'm in touch with these feelings; I know they are there, but I can't seem to let them out.

K: When there is so much grief, it is sometimes very threatening to allow ourselves free expression of our fear, sadness, anger, and despair. We may be afraid that if we feel and express it, we will either go mad or become stuck in interminable agony. It may be hard to trust it as a natural process which, by its very nature, moves. It is necessary to have a safe place to express these deep feelings. And, if they are to be shared, it must be with others who understand and are not afraid or judgmental. I have experienced this safety with a few close friends, in therapy, and in therapy groups. Attending a Life Transition workshop with Elisabeth Kübler-Ross, I was able to accelerate the healing process during the end of my marriage. I beat a mattress with a hose until I was exhausted. My whole body ached for a couple of days, but it was a relief to feel my pain this way rather than emotionally. The process of externalization, as Elisabeth calls it, enabled me to feel more relaxed than I had in years, certainly lighter and freer and ready to go on to the next adventure.

When my mother was dying, I felt a strong need to be held and comforted and had many beautiful friends who understood and were able to give this to me. I have not found nor used these resources during this time, and, consequently, I have had physical problems. I think that the loss of a mother may be easier to go through with a friend than impending widowhood. My experience as a therapist helps me understand and trust the process of grief, but it doesn't spare me the least bit of pain and hurt.

H: You speak of reaching out for support, the support of friends when you hit bottom. But I've never known or sought that kind of support. During so many dyings, I wouldn't have known whom to seek out, to whom to cry out, to be held, to be heard. Nor would I have wanted this support. I was in control and I guess I wanted it that way. You were safe. I was alone in the midst of danger, whistling, tying up all the loose ends, covering up grief with busy work. Why can't I reach out to others? Even to reach out to you, now, I find difficult.

K: I think you used the key word, *control*. It's hard to let go, particularly for a man. It makes me feel very sad that you have carried so much for so long. I am particularly moved by your finding it difficult even to reach out to me. I know what you mean. I am desperately trying to hold myself together, too, and you may sense this. I'm involved in my own grief process, and at times, I am unavailable. So, habit and individual need make this hard.

H: I think I understand, but I still wonder why you haven't needed the kind of comfort and support you sought so needfully during your mother's final illness and the death of your first marriage. Does my apparent stoicism prevent you from showing your deepest emotions? Would it be easier or harder for you if I were able to release my feelings of grief? Is it somehow easier for women to express their deepest feelings because men have been so socialized, brainwashed even, to deny deep emotion?

For example, my father expected me, even as a child, to be "brave" in the face of any pain or disappointment. To be "Spartan" was his greatest wish for me, in contrast to my mother who was, herself, emotionally expressive and encouraged such free expression of feelings in me. Several times, in my childhood, my father told me the story of the Spartan boy who wanted a wolf for a pet. His father told him he could not have one, but the boy defied him and stole a cub from the wolf's den. Holding the cub under his toga, he started for home but met his father on the way. As they stopped to talk, the cub began to gnaw at the boy's chest, but the boy, afraid of his father's anger, gave no sign of the pain and hurt the cub was inflicting. At last, the blood soaked through the toga and the father tore the cloth aside and flung the cub away. Anger? Retribution? No. The father's only words were, "My son, you are a true Spartan, and I am proud of you." I guess I'm still trying to live up to my father's Spartan creed. Could that story, those expectations, have so influenced the repression of what were considered "unmasculine" emotions? Is this what inhibits so many men from experiencing and revealing the full play of their feelings?

K: I've wondered about some of these same questions also. I have never been through this experience before, and I'm surprised by some of my reactions. Even though there is something so intimate, so private about this momentous event, here we are writing about it for others to see. It's true, I don't seem to need the same sort of support as I needed before. I seem to get comfort from the confidence of having survived some difficult times. We're focusing so much of our energy on the writing of this book, because the logjam within you is beginning to break up, and we have so much to say to each other. We always have had a lot to talk about and discuss. The first months and years together we got very little sleep—we were awake most of the night talking. Now, with this forced separation during the weeks you must be at the National Cancer Institute and I in Hartford, we are still talking, on the telephone and on paper. This is part of our grief process. It helps us express our feelings and thoughts in a uniquely personal and quiet way. This, and being apart while you are undergoing your therapy, has forced us inside ourselves.

Right now, as I read your questions, I am flying away from you back to our home in Hartford. My tears fall down my face as if a faucet were turned on as I glimpse your apartment building through the plane window. We climb into the clouds. I bless you down there as you may do me some day. Though our hearts are broken, we became silly today. I looked up from the word processor and said that all this writing is making me so sad. And you said, so matter-of-factly, "Well, sweetheart, this is a lot of sad stuff. What did you expect?" We began to laugh. I needed to come up for air.

H: Can this kind of release be a part of the grief process? Does it all have to be a progress from sorrow to rage, to depression, to fruitless bargaining, to the context of meaning, to understanding, to resolution, with no stops along the way for the relief of laughter, even if it is gallows humor?

K: Your cheerfulness and good humor have always been a delight to me except when they were a cover-up for no feelings at all. You are energetic, bright, clever, and funny with a sense of irony. I appreciate your unique personality. You make me laugh, cry, pull out my hair. It's a lot. You always spring back to this essential core, though, and I am used to it. I've often said that I wouldn't know what I'd do if you were depressed. I guess I could ask some of the same questions, but I really think we are doing what we need to do. You are giving yourself freedom to express your grief now, admitting your vulnerability, and I am getting closer to the real person who is there when the masks of denial, cleverness, and irony are torn away.

H: As I am increasingly able to get in touch with my deepest feelings, I find that the imminence of death focuses one's attention on those lessons one has learned in a lifetime that are beyond skills, talents, successes, or failures. I feel grief not in losing comforts or pleasures or even skills and accomplishments, but in losing, on this plane at least, the growing and deepening love we share, the chance to achieve truly open and honest relationships with all our children, and the chance, free of fetters, to find and nurture that filament of spirit Lewis Thomas writes about that joins all of us with the eternal core of being. But until that time of death, I feel more and more the need of nurture and support.

K: I know that. For you, that need is a difficult admission. In terms of support, I think of a triangle or a tepee. Sometimes there is not enough support with just the two of us leaning into each other. We need the loving, strong arms of our children joined with ours in one big, crying hug. We find our strength leaning together toward each other. I want you to have and to feel this protection we can give you. My children have been here for you and continue to be. Some of your children will have to learn for the first time that you, too, have needs. We must go through this together. Together, we must find the spiritual context of meaning that lets us both grieve and grow through this awe-filled event.

H: When I was a skeptical, know-it-all graduate student, I was appalled that so many intelligent, skeptical, rational human beings, men and women of great gifts of intellect and talent, converted to some form of Christianity in the face of death. I thought it was the ultimate cop-out. But now I realize that they were focused on their spiritual center, the place where rationality, irony, cleverness, and worldly preoccupation are without power or meaning. Institutional religion was one answer, in those days, perhaps the only spiritual refuge. When even the most rational human being, at the end, is on a search for his spiritual core, is that a sign that what you call the "transition" is at hand? Is that what I am experiencing now?

K: It seems that we focus on these important things only when challenged to do so. The Type A personality—the hard-driving and driven executive—changes his habits of exercise and diet when there is danger of heart attack. We are more concerned about the importance of healthy habits as we become more aware of our physical vulnerability in middle age. So it seems there is a turning toward the business at hand when we realize we are really dealing with mortality, and it is very serious. I've thought recently how strange it is that we turn to the so-called "alternative" therapies only in these times of dire need. Why, only now, have you had a consultation with a macrobiotic specialist, seeking a diagnosis and recommendation according to ancient Chinese methods? Why don't I, too, take this opportunity to consider some forms of prevention before it is too late? I watch someone eat a grinder sandwich and remember what it was like to have a youthful metabolism that could take all the calo-

ries, and a digestive system that could handle all that bolo-
gna and oil and fat. I took it for granted that I'd always be
eating grinders. That seems pretty trite in relation to your
thoughts about the great figures of reason turning to religion
at the end of their lives. Life so narrows down at its end.

We sat in a Japanese restaurant today and looked at the
men at the next table, dressed in blue business suits, postur-
ing importantly as if the business they were discussing was
vital. We remarked how ridiculous all that seems now to us
as we prepare to return to the National Cancer Institute for
the wrap-up, the no-news news that Suramin has provided
no benefit and has, instead, so compromised the strength in
your legs that you may always walk haltingly with a cane. It
puts things in a different perspective. A part of the grief is
the loss of the mundane. With this loss comes the pulling
away from us of people who cannot stand the emotional intensity and the constant reminder of what we all want to
forget. You and I no longer have the choice to avoid what
is happening to you. The other "great minds" whom you
mention realized that that choice was lost to them, too.
They needed a context of meaning for their grief over the
end of their lives, and they found it in a religion of certainty
that this life is not the end. And that all sins are forgiven.

H: I think, finally, I can unblock the denial and the control
and embark with you on the process of grieving for what is
lost and what can never be. But I still worry that what I feel
as a deep, spiritual experience is little more than self-pity. Is
self-pity part of the grief process? Do we have license to feel
sorry for ourselves in our dying?

K: Of course. Self-pity is a perfectly natural feeling at these times, a part of the process of grieving for yourself. I would expect you to feel this way. I feel sorry for us. Here we are, two energetic, talented, committed, humane people with so much left to discover and explore together. I cried at dinner last night because you understood so perfectly something I was saying. That's been so rare in my experience. You quickly catch on to what I am trying to say even when I am doing it awkwardly, almost incoherently. That's meant so much and now it will be taken away from me.

You know, there is this basic question we have as humans. It is this: What is going to happen to me? I respect this plaintive, basic cry. It might be hard to admit as an adult that it's in us, but it is. Our fear about this seems to be that if we give in to our feelings of self-sorrow, they will consume us. We sometimes interrupt the natural flow of feeling with suppression, repression, or denial. That's been your lifelong habit. When that happens, we get into trouble, sometimes stuck in the process. So it seems better to recognize these feelings, to experience them, and let them go. So many problems arise because we fight our basic nature. In the words of my beloved therapist Arne Welhaven, "As if our pea brains had a better idea than creation itself."

MEDITATION 8—THE SPIRITUAL JOURNEY

I had a dream, a dream while half awake. I think I had been reading Stephen Hawking, and the cosmos was weighing heavily upon me. Suddenly, a voice spoke to me, from within me—my voice, but the words seemed not my own.

And the voice said, "God is in you. God is of you. God is you." I felt humbled by this and I asked that God within, "Why did it all begin? The big bang. The whole universe"?

And the voice answered, "The beginning has been so trivialized by calling it 'The Big Bang.' Think of it as 'The Awakening.'" And I asked, "But why did you awaken? What disturbed your long sleep?" And the voice answered, "I dreamed of a garden."

I believe that this was a transcendent spiritual experience. I was deeply moved by it then, and as I recall it now, it still has the power to stir me. For I think that the dream of a garden launches a journey toward beauty and peace in all of us. It may be a literal garden. I remember the emotional power of seeing the poorest, most ramshackle homes in the barrios of San Antonio, ornamented with beautiful, well-tended flowers, even if they had to be limited to window boxes. I recall how I, no gardener, felt such kinship with the renewing earth as I scratched the scraggly grass of my lawn with a rake and could almost hear the earth stretch and sigh. Why does the symbol of the garden figure so prominently in the world's religions? Isn't it the loss of Eden that calls us to rebuild it in our own tiny backyard spaces?

I'm not quite sure what a "spiritual journey" is. Words like *spiritual* always seem so presumptuous to me, as if our life is something more than a journey through reality from birth to death. From time to time, and increasingly so since my own journey's destination seems so much closer, I have had, as in that dream, experiences which I suppose could be called spiritual. But I can't pretend that the voice was anything but my own and that the words were prompted by my hope and desire for universal beauty and meaning at this time.

I had another dream a few days ago. Because of increasing edema caused by the Suramin, I lay on the couch with my legs elevated and fell asleep reading a book on transcendental meditation. In my almost-sleep state, I asked for a mantra, a phrase, syllables, that would help me with my meditating. When I was completely asleep, I dreamed that I was in Lhasa, in Tibet. The monks in their saffron robes were twirling the prayer wheels. There were pennants flying and the sound of unison chanting. I felt a great happiness, a sense of bliss, in Joseph Campbell's words. And then, my mantra came to me. It was, "Nothing dies." Now, wherever I am, whatever I am doing, when I repeat these words, I can see immediately the whirling prayer wheels, the flapping pennants, hear the chanting of the monks, and I feel again the great happiness first experienced in the dream. Is this a spiritual experience, a message from beyond myself, or am I simply trying desperately to disguise the reality of the final ending with a hope for heaven? I must ask Kay.

CONVERSATION 8—THE SPIRITUAL JOURNEY

HERB: Even now, as I reach into myself for some greater meaning, some sense of larger purpose to my life, to all life, I'm still uncomfortable, out of my element, when I use the word *spiritual.* What do *you* mean by it? Why does it come so easily and naturally to you? Is it because Judaism, in which I had my religious training, seems so earthbound and ethically based that it has never informed me about my soul or spirit? I love the words of Micah: "What doth the Lord require of thee but to do justice, to love mercy, and to walk humbly with thy God"—but that is a guide for conduct in *this* world. It tells me nothing of a realm beyond this, and the Christ-centered myths and rituals of Christianity are simply not available to me. How, then, can I find the spiritual core I am so avidly seeking as the dying process carries me along?

KAY: It seems to me that you are both asking and answering this question yourself. Your spiritual journey is evolving more and more, and you are finding answers within yourself. Even though you are not certain that they are the right answers, you are gaining trust and confidence in pursuing your inner journey. At least, you seem certain there is one and that it is real and important to you.

I think I've said before that sometimes people with gifted intellect do not find enough logical substance, enough scientific data to launch a serious discussion of the spiritual experience of dying and death. Sometimes there is an arrogance associated with the overdependence on reason, and with science's insistence on using data that can be perceived, measured, predicted, and repeated. To me, this is an all-too-literal interpretation of relationships and events. What is so gratifying to me is what I believe is your genuine discovery, on your own, of an inner world by just following a process of deeper thought and curiosity. Your ability to see beauty in facing death, of being moved by it, is a recognition of the preciousness of this experience. This is a whole other lens, a deeper sensory experience not limited by a strictly logical structure. It has given added breadth and depth to your recognition of a limited life span.

H: But for you, the discovery of the spiritual seems to have come as naturally, as easily, as the rational, logical dimension of your mind. How do you account for this when it has taken me so long to find it within myself?

K: From earliest childhood, I was curious about the meaning of life. I sensed the awful discrepancy between fairness and what actually happens in this world. I knew that justice and fairness had to be absolute values of the human experience, but I knew that for countless millions, they were not to be found here. I felt injured as a child and had in me the feeling that there existed somewhere, something just. My religious training taught me that this was God. And to sustain that perspective as a child, I felt a piety and was attracted to the more ritualistic practice of religion as an expression of what seemed holy to me. And I developed the conviction that there had to be something more not seen, not here, but at the very core of the universe.

I think that because, out of loneliness, I spent a lot of time in an imaginary world, I felt comfortable in imagining a more loving and just world to escape the loneliness and pain. And it was easy for me to conceive of a realm not seen and experienced by physical reality or logic. I had a sense of an ultimate reality in which God loved me. I was cared for, important. I mattered. And from this I came to realize that this reality was not just for me in my loneliness. It applied to everyone. And I always felt that our empirical experience is not enough.

H: Out of loneliness, I, too, lived much of my childhood in an imaginary world of my own creation—but it never developed a larger, spiritual dimension. It amounted to little more than an exercise of the creative imagination. Bringing toys to life. Writing stories and poems of imaginary events but never relating this experience to a larger, less egocentric world view.

K: As a teenager walking home from choir practice, I remember telling my best friend, Barbara, that I wanted to be a missionary. She said she wanted to be a newspaper reporter, which I found uninspiring at that time. I told her that life had to matter. That it wasn't enough to live it on the surface. There had to be something more than pursuing one's pleasures and interests. That a sense of purpose and responsibility and mission was the reason we are here, not a random accident. Of course, Barbara was the one to become a missionary in the Bowery, while I became a housewife. I had the church's rituals to help me understand this when I was a child. As an adult I found the church lacking in the expression of the deeper spirit, and so with curiosity and perseverance, I studied theology. Through that effort and contact with uniquely beautiful, committed people to guide me, especially my friend Jean, I found both love and an interpretation of my experience in terms of the spirit.

H: And you didn't lose this sense of spirit as you became weighted down with children, husband, home, and all the minutiae of everyday existence?

K: During the sixties and seventies, sensitivity training helped me meld my individual experiences with those of others, and that brought together within me the realms and disciplines of individual psychology and spirituality. Unlike you, I always had an understanding of Jesus Christ as an expression of the divine human dimension that is in all of us. Through my interest in George Fox and the Quakers, I came to the certainty that we all have the divine light within us. We are all redeemed and saved. We are all holy at the essential core of our being. And I feel that that perception of the Christ within is what makes our own spiritual journeys, yours and mine, so different.

When I began the chaplaincy program, I had that special experience that seemed to guide me. I truly felt I was being guided. Finally, I had reached the place where I was supposed to be, doing work I had, as an adolescent, dreamed of doing. It is this divine aspect in which each one of us is held—call it the lap of the goddess, the hand of God—each religion or myth has its own description of a place where we are safe and at peace.

H: You seem to place so much emphasis on the feeling of safety in approaching death. Does this depend on one's confidence in doctors, therapies, and drugs, or is it some deeper awareness of being protected from harm?

K: This is the most important information I have to share with my patients and clients and with you. And I know that it's hard for you, after a lifetime of skepticism, of belief in the ultimate power of reason and logic, to give up your defenses of the mind and brain and to enter the simpler, more subjective realm of the spirit. But confronting your own death clears away a lot of tangled underbrush you've accumulated over the years. I sense that you are fully convinced that you have embarked on a new and deeper kind of journey, a journey that you accept on its own terms, not one that you have taken before. We must compensate for our unnatural fear of death with the reminder of the safety of the natural process.

H: I accept that, and the journey as I see it, is the attempt to locate the spirit, my spiritual core, through all the veils of reason, doubt, skepticism, and scientific rationalization. Two years ago, there were barriers I could not have struck down. They defined me, my beliefs, my understanding of reality and the human condition. I took great pride both in my secular humanism and my liberal humanitarianism. The word *spiritual* was one I was never motivated to use. How do you evoke the spiritual in yourself and others, apart from your own conviction and example? Does it take approaching death to get most people even to admit that they are now open to this journey into the dimension of the spiritual?

K: Oh, yes. In so many ways this work is easy, because all I need to do is confirm something of which people are consciously or preconsciously aware. Working with persons near death is easy in this way, because they seem to have a strong, certain knowledge of ultimate reality—as I perceive this happening to you. My work has become a matter of sharing what my clients and teachers have taught me, built upon my own intuitive base of which I spoke earlier.

H: I've always thought that the ultimate journey in life is toward the "truth," and that the truth can only be grasped through the mind, the brain, the rational self. How does the journey of the spirit differ from the quest for the "truth"? Is there a truth that we can grasp on this side of the grave with our limited, finite capacity to understand the infinite? With what Arne Welhaven called our "pea brains"?

K: It's not something you can arrive at through intellectualization. It's not possible to convince people through rational discourse and argument. The knowledge and the conviction are not easily transmitted. How could I convince you that at the heart of this insignificant speck of dust is a core of the divine? All knowledge, and I'm talking about certainty, not faith, has had to come from somewhere. How do you arrive at a truth? Now that you've begun to experience the difference between mastering a fact and exploring ultimate reality, how does it seem to you? Do you see now what a limitation it is to try to get at ultimate reality—that is so enormously wide and all-encompassing—by limiting yourself to scientific method and logic? How can you limit your understanding to the mind? We are surrounded by so many mysteries, so many veils that have not been pierced by all our science, all our reason. As death approaches, the sense of the infinite seems to open up, and what has seemed to be fantasy now seems real. Ultimate truth cannot be considered in such a limited fashion. As if we could figure it all out, understand all the mystery with such a limited tool as the reason, even though this way of thinking about reality may make the most sense to us, be the most rational and reasonable. It's like trying to look at the Grand Canyon at midnight with dark glasses on.

H: But trying to describe the meaning of death and what comes after *is* like looking at the Grand Canyon at midnight. What we have to work with is so feeble, so limited. At least that's the way I feel. I don't think I could possibly describe, with my limited experience, what continues after death.

K: You use the word *feeble* in describing our instrument. That seems not to show enough respect for the inner divine nature's ability to recognize its reality. The infinite is, by definition, wonder, inconceivable majesty, ultimate beauty and possibility. How do we understand these mysteries? What continues after death? I believe it is that divine part in all of us. I don't know what else continues of our individual selves. My image is that there is a cluster of unifying, identifying aspects of our being, so that just as we are identifiable here, a pattern that unites all the billions of cells and bits of energy and matter of which we are built remains identifiable for some time until it merges again with divine nature. And that is what we mean by spirit.

I believe we have intimations of this in our dreamworlds. How is it that when we dream at night we inhabit this strange landscape, this world of dreams, and when we awaken, we can consider the dream as a perfectly natural experience? The experience of altered states of consciousness gives us the awareness of a world other than the physical world we customarily inhabit. When we dream, we are in the world of the spirit, yet it is perfectly natural to have a dream and wake up and understand that it was a dream. It doesn't make it any less real because of the difference in perspective. So we know about other states of being and perceiving that don't require our bodies. Knowing all of that, it's easy for me to believe that when the body dies, there is a divine, infinite core and cluster of identifiable characteristics that continue beyond the door. Certainly, all the research on near-death experiences verifies this understanding. In almost every case, the persons near death retain their identity on the mysterious passage to the light, and the departed loved ones who are there to greet them are recognizable and identifiable. It's really interesting that we can so naturally integrate these unusual experiences into our consciousness.

When I first spoke to my mother about near-death experiences, she told me that years before she had had one. She was bleeding internally and very near death. She knew she had to come back and take care of the baby she had given birth to. A voice said to her, "Not yet. Not yet. You have to go back and take care of the baby." I was that baby. She never mentioned the experience to anyone, because she thought she would not be believed. Yet now, we are comfortable with such experiences. We do not consider them strange or evidence of mental illness. She feared that the world would think her crazy, hearing voices like that. She stressed that the experience seemed entirely natural to her, and that she had no doubt of its truth.

H: If I could find some "context of meaning" in my dying, I guess I would have an easier time turning away from the mundane and focusing inward. Maybe that is still to come. But right now, I can't seem to get beyond my feeling of such unnecessary waste of a still-productive life because a careless, inefficient doctor missed the call until it was too late. Am I stuck in a part of the grief process that is inhibiting my spiritual development? Am I really asking the whining question I have always scorned, "Why me?"

K: It is so natural to ask this question. Yesterday we spoke to a young man who is dying of AIDS at age thirty-one. He was filled with the same feelings, the same questions. The same search for fairness and justice in this world. How can it be any other way if you love life and people? If you have interests, curiosities, and purposes? If you are very alive to the world, you must ask "Why?" And, of course, we are always forced painfully back to the fact that our physical existence is only temporary, filled with injustice, unfairness, and difficulty. And so it forces us to get beyond the limitations of our physical existence. It gives us the opportunity to discover and explore the internal world of the spirit.

The reality, though some of us are slower to realize it than others, is that we are embarked on a spiritual journey from the moment we are born. Our dying makes us more poignantly aware of it. Especially our dying before we have fulfilled what we thought of as our own purpose in this life. You, at almost the allotted three score and ten, still have "miles to go before you sleep." The young man dying at thirty-one had many more miles, many more dreams and desires. But in you both, the question, "Why me?" is a natural cry to the core of mystery within us. And the answer, I believe, is "Wait. There's an infinity to come."

H: How easy it has been to give up, to let go of work, achievement, goals, business, all the temporal activities and occupations that filled my life with activity, and essentially defined who I was to myself and the world. This is also true of the peripheral activities that once made up a "social life." I am sorry about this, because it means I am dragging you, too, into isolation and loneliness. But physical and psychic limitations have forced me into a state where I seem to want only peace, solitude, beauty, and a chance to reflect. In other words, a "garden." Even much of reading, of television, of keeping up with the world, has lost its power to illuminate, soothe, entertain, and distract. Am I entering a new stage of existence where, without realizing it, I am already on my spiritual journey through a whole new landscape of thought and feeling?

K: You speak of the spiritual journey as if it were a train that pulls into the station, and you are only now getting on. I guess you think of me as some sort of conductor on this train. I don't see it that way at all. This is the train you got on when you were born. Maybe now it's slowing down a little because for most of your life, you forced the train to travel at top speed, where the view from the windows was only a blur. How much has it taken to shock you out of that high-speed world in which real events were all that counted; in which several newspapers had to be read every day; television news watched; radio's *All Things Considered* a must just at dinnertime. And then you had to think and talk about what you had read and listened to. Ideas. Ideas. Ideas. Never time for quiet reflection. Life was too full, too crowded with deadlines, assignments, and challenges. And of course, you were doing all that so you wouldn't experience the terrible emptiness you feared was at the core of your being. Spiritual emptiness.

Everything in your life had to be crowded. Doubled. At top speed. Seven children to care for. Four jobs when I met you. Four families to support. Two residences. Two places of work. Two elderly mothers for whom you took full responsibility, one of whom with a perfectly able daughter to care for her. But you seemed to need to fill every minute, fill the whole stage with frenetic energy.

H: But that was all I knew how to do—to be used up by this world with no thought of a realm of spirit that would give me peace and some sort of continuity.

K: That's right. If this world is all there is, you seemed to say, I want to crowd everything into it. You were redeemed only by activity, responsibility, running faster, and carrying a heavier burden than anyone else. Now, to continue your train metaphor, you are looking out the window and seeing, finally, what is out there. And as your train is slowing down, you are seeing that not all of the scenery has been beautiful and wonderful. You have had to confront some very painful places that you sped by trying to avoid. You are pondering the emptiness and thinking about it in terms of a context of meaning. You felt once that you had to do it all, to be all, and now that the train has slowed down, as it does for so many, you are able to see your life in terms of your dying, and to find that context for yourself.

H: I only wish I had been able to reflect on these issues earlier in life. In my world there was no teacher, no guidance, no insight into the meaning of life and death.

K: It is so wonderful that so many people, young and old, are crowding university and high-school courses in death and dying. They are getting what you missed until you, yourself, were on the threshold of dying. Now, you are really taking a significant, courageous step to change your life. You can't think about death and dying without changing your life. It makes it so much easier to face fear, to face the inevitable question, "Why me, now?" Now you think you are safe and can come to a place where there is nothing to fear. It makes such a difference in the quality of your living and in the quality of your dying.

H: The Tibetan monks in my dream vision spend their lives in prayer. Strange that I have not yet found the need or the ability to pray—to pray for a cure, remission, more time than the year once predicted, or even to pray that I succeed in finding my spiritual center. Whom do you pray to? Certainly not the anthropomorphic God of the Old Testament, or even to His great prophets? Today, I did pray for the surcease of the pain you have from shingles. I threw my anguished cry into a diffuse void crowded with spirit and caring, I felt, but not to be defined. How does prayer function for you in times of pain and sorrow?

K: I think it's a matter of definition. What is prayer? Sitting down and praying in church to a patriarchal God image? You pray all the time, in a sense. At this moment, we are in New Mexico, in some ways closer to the spiritual world of the Indians, and you, a hundred times during the day, utter a prayer of thanksgiving for the beautiful sight of warm adobe against blue sky, a splash of yellow aspen on the mountains. These are all prayers of gratitude and thankfulness. I don't think you think of them as being prayers. But as the Indians of the Southwest did, in them you express a sense of wonder and reverence. Wouldn't you agree with the Lord's Prayer? Aren't there words you utter even in an informal way? Like the Twenty-third Psalm, or some poetry that is like a prayer. You say them to me. Some who meditate believe that life is itself a prayer. The monks are told to pray without ending.

H: And that is what you've told me. You have felt since earliest childhood that life is holy. That prayer is heard.

K: I can't say that prayer is heard. So often it seems not to be. But I can say that it matters. This is consistent with the fact of our significance and importance. We must pray. We must hold before us the image we wish to attain. Right now, I'm absorbed in my grief. You are far less angry at what is happening to you than I am. You will die at your allotted three score and ten. I'm feeling sorry for myself knowing that at age fifty-six, I'll have been divorced, orphaned, and probably widowed. My children are unable to bring new life into the family as yet. Nothing is as I imagined it to be at this time in my life, and I am having a hard time with that. I am feeling robbed of something I expected and thought would be mine.

I feel the same as the young man dying of AIDS. Life is not turning out the way we expected it to be. I feel very weighted down and angered at the material world. Since so much responsibility rests fully on my shoulders, my life has been crowded by you. And when you say you feel guilty for dragging me along into isolation, even if it is a garden, I feel frightened by that, because this space is going to leave an enormous void when you're gone.

It's not what I wanted to have happen to my marriage. After my divorce, I imagined a marriage in which I would never again become lost and my needs be neglected because those of my husband and my family were greater. And with the women's movement, I believed I could maintain an emotional identity separate and apart from a life role as wife.

That was quickly shattered at the beginning of our marriage by a series of traumatic events in your family that were to follow with regularity right up until now. It's a struggle, and I haven't always been able to do it very well. So I think I have a lot from which to recover. Even now we are living life according to your terms, and I feel that I am being consumed only to be regurgitated as some unrecognizable mass when it's all over. This is expressing it dramatically, but this is how it feels at its worst—that I will not be able to gather the pieces together, to begin again, when you are gone. Even though I know that isn't true, it's how it feels most of the time.

My father, whom we cared for during a series of medical crises during the previous two years, died in August, two months ago. At the same time, we found out that your treatment had failed and you were seriously ill with pneumonia and Legionnaires' disease. It was a time of grief and loss for me. After that, I experienced a week of excruciating pain from shingles, six weeks of intermittent neurological pain, the most severe pain I have ever experienced. My world is so full of you I can hardly bear to think about your not being here to fill my life in stressful and distressing ways, but also you are my best friend, someone with whom to share my thoughts and ideas and experiences. I can't imagine not having these conversations, your voice—you here talking with me. I don't know how I'll live without you. You will leave a huge, empty space in my life.

My prayers at the moment are to be able to get through each day, putting one foot in front of the other. I am in a state of anticipatory bereavement. I know you are going to be fine. You will die unafraid and resolved about your life. You will enter your garden. But I am looking ahead to a lot of loneliness, and right now, all I can feel is anguish about that. As you go more and more into your spiritual journey, I am forced to embark on that fast train where practical events and activities dominate. My spiritual journey has been interrupted, though I know that some time—in some way—my own "context of meaning," once so certain, will be restored. We are coming as close to spiritual attunement as we can and continually returning to the knowledge, even when it seems so remote, of ultimate goodness and love of God.

When I visited my mother's and father's graves, I saw them appear before me a few feet off the ground, looking young, whole, and happy, and they said, "Everything is all right." I realized again, weightiness is here on earth. You will be free.

MEDITATION 9—THE POWER OF LOVE

When you come right down to it, very little is left, at the end, except the memory of old love and the need and the capacity for present love every moment of every day.

The body, slowly sinking into its mortality, knows the futility of hate, the corrosiveness of stress; in fact, the emptiness of so many operatic emotions that blow like squalls through everyone's everyday life.

I think about all this because, by quirk of fate, I have been enabled by the course of this disease, and especially the more radical elements of its treatment, to have what is probably the most ferocious rage of all, sex, peeled away from love and totally removed from body, glands, emotions, and even memory.

Cut out by the surgeon's knife have been prostate and testicles. Destroyed by hormones and chemicals has been the testosterone that powered what in me was a constant, blazing presence for so much of my life.

Without these physical stimulators of the sex drive, sex is dead. It cannot even be remembered. Manifestations of sex in books, or films, or photographs, are totally without the power to stimulate recall. It is the way a person views a sign printed in an unfamiliar typeface in a totally unknown language. The symbols are all there, but they are without power or meaning.

What does this say to me? That sex has very little to do with love? That it is a purely biological drive connected to chemistry and not to spirit? No. Sex uses love to further its own single vital purpose, to drive the organisms toward the mating of male and female, toward the union that leads to procreation. This is certainly no ignoble mission, and if we have ennobled sex and confused desire with love in whose image it so often disguises itself, this is as nature intended. Sex creates that cauldron of intimacy between man and woman in which love and desire are fused. But because of the total extirpation of sex within me by surgeon's knife and chemical destroyer, I am in a unique position to see and feel the separation of the two.

Clearly, sex is of the body and not of the spirit, although, in its fusion of love and desire, it can open windows to the soul. Old men who recall past sexual prowess with fading delight are prompted by the last whispers of testosterone in their blood. And when that is gone, no power on earth can restore or renew the ecstatic rage that once dominated their lives.

But love cannot be removed by chemistry or scalpel. It has a totally different source and occupies a realm unconnected to the vicissitudes of the body or the mind. I think about and yearn for love continuously. A kind word spoken has the power to move me to tears. A memory of past love is as fresh and alive as the memory of old sex is dead and gone. I can bring to vivid life the love that propelled past acts of sex, even though trying to recall the emotional content of the acts themselves is futile, erased.

With love—and by *love* I mean the need and desire to give myself over to someone or something beyond myself—I approach what I perceive to be the realm of the spirit. And I feel sustained and comforted by this knowledge. But how and whether I can harness this power to healing or cure I do not know. I must ask Kay.

CONVERSATION 9—THE POWER OF LOVE

HERB: Since I wrote the Meditation on the Power of Love in July 1991, several months ago, so much has happened emotionally that I feel quite different now from the way I felt then. It is as if I have undergone a spring thaw, melting and cracking the ice that has held my deepest emotions immobilized, frozen—emotions that seem to be a part of a process that is the opposite of the full range of the process of grieving. It has resulted in an overwhelming rush of warmth, empathy, and caring that embraces everyone, everything. It's like the song (and we all know the power of cheap music) that goes, "There's a smile on my face for the whole human race, why it's almost like being in love." Even the tears that I shed, and they come frequently, are not tears of grief or frustration, but the satisfying tears that accompany genuine feeling. Have you ever experienced this phenomenon in other dying patients or clients? What is it? How does it function for me at this stage of the process?

KAY: In your meditation you were speaking about being liberated from the drives of your hormones, and how that liberation has allowed you to focus on other things with greater intensity than before. In these months, you have experienced heightened perceptions which have been shown through a greater sensitivity and openness to other people, a deeper appreciation of the environment and what it has to offer you, and an expansion of spiritual awareness.

It always seems amazing to find that there are things to be gained in the midst of such hideous loss. That is why some people who have had cancer say that the disease is the best thing that ever happened to them. These are called secondary gains. In therapy, we try to discover what the disease is enabling people to do so that they might be able to achieve the same goals without needing the disease. We attempt to find ways of accomplishing those ends at a less drastic cost. We don't want to need the disease. The idea is to make conscious any somatic effects and empower the psyche instead. The functional aspect of disease is very interesting and important to consider in terms of one's healing. It was my impression initially that your illness helped you consider whole realms hitherto avoided, dismissed, or thought unnecessary.

The work you so earnestly have done in trying to resolve conflicted relationships, healing past injuries, and more honestly sharing your feelings with others has contributed to the uncluttered expansiveness you now experience. It seems that we are full of the clutter of all these things that seem so important so much of the time, until some shocking trauma puts everything back into perspective. It seems like such a waste not to have time to think and feel and sense the really essential things of life. But that's what we seem to do. It is the tragedy of your life that in order to liberate this feeling of love, you had to develop an irreversible disease that robbed you of the sexual expression of it. This is my tragedy, too.

This global, generalized feeling of love seems to come with the hard work of struggle and from spiritual openness along with physical changes. Your life is considerably more simple since you retired and have been at home.

I have a visualization exercise which I will describe later in detail. You enter a cave on whose wall is a message specially written for you. When I first did this exercise many years ago, my special words were, "You are not alone." My friend, Jean's message was the word *love*. I believe the appropriate words or message are within each one of us. It often seems so hard to become still enough or disciplined enough to listen to that message.

I remember a small plaster plaque that hung in the front room of my grandmother's house in West Virginia. Because I admired it so often, before she died, she gave the plaque to me. It was kind of corny I guess, but it had special appeal to me. I thought it was very beautiful. It said, simply, GOD IS LOVE. As we grow spiritually, we grow in the spirit of love. Now you are finding that your feelings, which you are able to express more freely and openly, are permeated with feelings of love. You feel loved and accept your feelings without being judgmental. You have the satisfaction of a purity of feeling with no ambiguity or ambivalence in it. It is pure feeling and the experience is very full and satisfying, whether the feeling is sadness, grief, anger, or regret. There is no need to try to rechannel difficult emotions into more acceptable feelings. It is easier to be honest about that.

H: Last night I was watching a movie on TV called *The Divided Heart*. I hadn't really connected with the story, but I knew it was about a young boy, separated from his Yugoslavian mother as a baby during World War II and rescued from certain death by a young German woman who nurtured him for ten years. Then, he is rediscovered by his birth mother, who petitions the Allied Command to have him returned to her. As soon as she entered the apartment of his foster parents, I began to sob, not in sadness, but as a kind of reunion with my own birth mother whom I lost when I was seventeen. There was such a feeling of release, of connectedness, of love long denied. Am I now able to express feelings I've kept buried for so long? Is the real power of this love to help propel me more willingly to the other side?

K: Yes, it seems to be. Trust the feeling you have about it. You are making a powerfully healing connection with your mother, who is on the other side of death, reestablishing a bond that had been severed for so long. When you watched that movie, you were having a reunion with your true mother, having acceded to your father's demand that you pretend that Dora was your only mother and to deny for years, until just recently in fact, that your birth mother played such an important, albeit tragic, part in your life. You must have known emotionally that this was a terrible thing to ask, but you kept up the pretense for years long after both Dora and your father died. Through a reawakening of love for your mother, a love you haven't experienced in so long, you were resolving a very significant piece of unfinished business that has haunted your life.

H: In my meditation, I spoke of the hormonal, glandular, somatic source of sexual love which has long been stripped from me. And I contrasted it with what remains when the testosterone is stopped, when female hormones are added to the mix, and I said that I felt that what remained as residue was a generalized feeling of love, a need for love, more pure than that stimulated by libido. I realize now that this dualistic, mind-body schematic is wrong. Love—to reach for it, to explore it, ultimately to find it—is the very unitary root and core of our being. It is why we are alive, why we create life. It is both the dancer and the dance.

True, sexual love, the libido, and the urge to reproduce, are one aspect of love, the way the earth replenishes itself. But at the end, the need and desire to love and be loved are just as strong with or without hormones or the libido. Is this what we mean by "spirituality," becoming one with the spirit of love that seems to be at the heart of all things?

K: What to me is so beautiful is that you are trusting your experience and letting it flow. That's where the beauty and the power of love have their fullest expression, to be authentic and to feel the fullness and richness of emotions long forgotten. The only way we can have the capacity to feel deep love is if we can also feel deep anger, sorrow, and doubt. Feeling free to express the whole range of our emotions expands our capacity to love. Somehow, we've created a culture in which we prize the constriction of emotions, not their full expression. Passion is to be avoided, and yet passionate people have a range and depth of emotion that puts them closer to the core source of universal feeling, and that is where you are now.

My grandmother's plaque said, GOD IS LOVE. Love is all. This is the other side of the Buddhist belief that as we approach God, we are absorbed not into the fullness of love but the emptiness of nirvana. Each concept of ultimate reality is the "all." Now, as you approach your personal death, you are dealing with ultimate matters and expanding your consciousness into areas you hadn't been able to reach before. For you, the answer after death lies not in a global loss of consciousness, but a total consciousness, suffused with love, that knows no definition or limitation. And of this, you were totally unconscious before the process of dying, before the spiritual journey began.

H: As time goes by, I become less and less able to tolerate violence of any kind—verbal, physical, or recreational. I can't watch TV scenes of battles, of cruelty, of verbal slurs or physical abuse inflicted on others. I find it devastating when you become angry at me. It feels like the end of the world and of me. Dylan Thomas urges his dying father not to "go gentle into that good night. Rage, rage against the dying of the light." I want to do just the opposite—to merge blissfully, lovingly with the loving source I now feel so strongly is at the core of the universe, its context of meaning. Have you experienced this with others who were dying? And what has your role been in helping to make this come about?

K: This is part of the process of letting go of the things of this world. You are more sensitive and vulnerable. Everything is magnified, expanded, especially those emotions and events that are anchored in the world you are going to leave behind. Now, you feel all emotions with greater sensitivity and reject those that have no bearing on your journey. When you speak of violence, I think about what your treatment has done to you. The disease is violent enough, but what would your life be like if you hadn't taken the experimental protocol? None of the National Cancer Institute protocols have been successful, but have added to your problems. Your treatment is partly responsible for your compromised physical condition, and it has affected your quality of life. It is the violence of your treatments that is terrifying to me, because it is an unnatural process. I have been enraged over these unnecessary compromises. You've experienced so much violence in your body, maybe this is also a source of your particular sensitivity to all violence. I think I presented the merging image to you and you now recognize it as your own.

H: I do regret deeply—feel miserable, in fact—the ending of sexual capacity. But—and this is hard to admit—its loss has made possible the release of a gentler, more spiritual, less sharply focused source and expression of love. I am enveloped in feelings of love that are a balm, not a fire. It is such a gift that it overwhelms regret, self-pity, or even grief, though it lets me grieve for you. Is this the "still small voice" that comes after the raging storm, to use the Biblical metaphor?

K: Remember that the object of all spiritual life that incorporates celibacy is to rid oneself of the sexual drive, to refocus this energy on the love of God with all one's being. The loss of sexual capacity has functioned for you in some ways. It has been good for me in some ways, too, as it has made you such an easier person to live with. You are less driven and more accepting.

The loss of sexual activity which played such a strong part in our relationship has been devastating to me. I ask myself if I will ever be in a sexual relationship again. I feel that I am dying, too, that my sexual life is dead. This may not be true, but it feels like it. My anger is expressed in a kind of turning off. It doesn't function the same for me as for you, because I don't have the disease. It's why I have put on weight, eaten the wrong foods to satisfy myself physically. Food has taken the place of sex.

This whole thing started with your occasional impotence that you denied, ignored, avoided until it was too late to do something about it. Your doctors, all of them, said it was a natural function of aging, and when you realized how unsatisfactory this answer was, the cancer had already metastasized. If the cause of the symptoms had been recognized when I was complaining to you about it, it could have been different. I knew something was wrong but the "experts" wouldn't listen to me, nor would you. That is why it is so important to pay attention to symptoms. Now, it's my problem to resolve. Denial did you in. You can't go from a very active sexual life to no sex at all without something being wrong. But you pretended it was not happening, and now, as you feel a great generalized love, I feel rage.

H: What I have written about these new feelings of love almost contradicts the title we chose for this conversation—The Power of Love. If these feelings are so gentle, so calm, what is love's power? Is it the power to rob death of its terror and loneliness because it so strongly suggests a joining and not a separation?

K: It's so beautiful, the way you express it. You are describing a gentler love, but there is a powerful love directed toward those people and things you feel deeply about. This is the love that sustained some people through the Holocaust—the determination to survive because life was so important, so much to be held on to. This is the power of love.

H: And what of your feelings of love—for me, specifically, as I move into a different part of the stream of life? Are you impatient with my dying so that you can, hopefully, experience sexual love, passion, before it's too late? Can you now tune into that flow that I was able to discover only when I knew I was dying?

K: Love has resulted in so much pain for me. It has taken so much away. I know I will continue and I am better equipped to live than before because I've had so much more experience with both happiness and suffering. I really like being married, yet I can't think of a relationship with another man. The kind of relationship I want requires so much. I don't seem to have the capacity to take men into my life simply for sex. I want it all. I know that a middle-aged woman can survive, can make it alone. Women are incredibly adaptable. But right now, in many ways, I feel like a big breast. I feel used up by all the men in my life who have expected and demanded that I nurture them without my being nurtured in return in my role as wife, mother, daughter, and sister. I now experience constant pain that shoots right through my heart, right through my breast. The symbolism is clear to me. Love and nurture have created pain in me. I've been shot through the heart and breast with love's arrow. This is the difference in the way we are feeling. The eros of love has been transferred to me, the agape to you as you face death in a rush of love.

H: Physical love, desire, attraction have their price in pain and frustration. It would be utterly insufferable of me to minimize your pain and your frustration and try to explain smugly the virtue of being a eunuch. But still, in the natural process of living, the fire of passion in each of us is tamped down, and what was once a searing drive becomes a more spiritual, deeper intimacy. Isn't this what lies at the source of all being?

K: Yes, that's why the natural process of living, as you call it, is so beautiful. So much to be trusted. That is what counters the Hemlock Society, which would intervene in the natural process. At every stage, even through suffering, the potential for love is always there. Look at the severely disabled child who asks everything of us; who every day tests our love, who absolutely requires that we learn how to grow, how to love, how to live. That's what it's all about. I'm imperfect in my love right now, but that's all right. It is to be beyond the egocentric predicament, to have a glimpse of wholeness, even if it seems impossible to attain. People like you, near death, certainly have a better sense of that. The goal of my work is to teach people to trust the process, to give assurance that dying and death, like all of life and what comes after, are holy events which need to take place in an atmosphere of love, given and received.

H: And so the end of the grief process, too, is the discovery that love overcomes loss, and the final reconciliation is with the fact that, as I dreamed when I asked my Tibetan monks for a mantra, it was—"Nothing dies."

K: Yes.

MEDITATION 10—HOME, HOSPITAL, HOSPICE

During the three months of Karyl's dying, we tried to make her living as comfortable and familiar as possible. After a period of recovery from surgery at the hospital, we brought her home by ambulance. In our bedroom, next to the Viking oak double bed we had shared for thirty-eight years, we placed an electrically operated hospital bed.

The next room, which our daughters had shared in their early years, we turned into a comfortable sitting room for Karyl, when she felt up to it, and for the private-duty nurses who cared for her around the clock. We installed a small refrigerator for the pain-controlling medications methadone and Thorazine, which only the nurses could administer.

For a month or more, this arrangement worked well. Friends could visit her upstairs. Downstairs, in the mother-in-law suite we had built for her, her mother, growing more embittered and angry every day, could hold her own Court of Complaints. It was such an effort for her to climb the stairs that her visits with Karyl were infrequent.

Then, as Karyl's cancer-choked stomach became less able to keep down food, we had to rush her back to the hospital. When the violent retching was once again controlled by drugs, she wanted to return home to die, and so, it was back by ambulance. This time, the ambulance was met by a crowd of friends and neighbors who greeted her and expressed their deep sorrow and affection for her. That moment meant so much to Karyl that even though she had to return to the hospital two days later, just before Christmas, the outpouring of neighborly love sustained her in the three weeks that remained of her life.

Now, August 1991, earlier on the very day I am writing this, I have been told bluntly but kindly that all hormone therapy has failed and that I have only a few months to live. This gives great importance, if not urgency, to the subject of the surroundings of my final dying and my death. Having no direct experience of the hospice concept, I know it only from what I have read and what Kay has told me about it. I appreciate its attention to the alleviation of pain and to the creation of an affirming, sustaining environment in the days of final transition. My fear is, however, that its finality, if one is aware of it, signals the death of all hope, all options to live.

As to hospitals, I have had so much experience with them in these past two years that they do not frighten me. For the most part, I have found them to be places of warm and consistent caring. And if there were a palliative-care team approach and a sensitivity to the special needs of the dying, I would not oppose the hospital as the terminus of the final journey.

It is when I think of dying at home that I am most torn and troubled. Haven't I caused enough chaos in that beautiful place of peace and repose? Didn't I start out with my desk in the bedroom, windows removed for bookshelves, extra telephone lines, a television where there once had been quiet? Do I have the right to create even more chaos with hospital bed and nurses' station and all the paraphernalia and sadness that accompany the final chapter?

I would like, at the end, to be able to see the tree outside the bedroom window, to sit or lie on the flower-filled sun porch, and, whatever the season, to look out on the garden with its statue of calm, serene Buddha at its center. I would like to have Kay near, to enjoy the last quiet moments with my dog and cat, to feel that children and friends, if they wanted to visit, could come to the place of beauty that Kay, with a little bit of me, had shaped.

Home, hospital, hospice—unless I am carried away suddenly and sooner—there should be time to make a choice. But wherever, and whenever, the time is at hand, I would like to feel I had a part in the decision. Maybe I am making too much of what will be a choice that almost makes itself. I must ask Kay.

CONVERSATION 10—HOME, HOSPITAL, HOSPICE

HERB: I feel that the issue of where I'm going to die is as important to me right now as when I'm going to die. Unless some quick and lethal pneumonia or stroke carries me off unexpectedly, I'm assuming that the disease will maintain a relatively slow, downhill course, permitting me the luxury (if it can be called that) of a choice of where to die. Home, hospital, hospice. What should be the factors that enter into the decision? Do you have any feelings now about what such a decision should be when the time comes?

KAY: Where to die? I think of the deathbed scenes in books and movies from prehospital death times. The central focus of these scenes is the massive bed, the dying one propped up with lots of pillows; the soft glow of candlelight creating an aura of holiness; the chamber filled with solemn, praying people, loved ones ministering to the needs of the one who is dying; friends and acquaintances lined up for final farewells; and relatives eager to hear the last words and to witness the passage of the soul into heaven. This sacred place near the one who is becoming holy because of proximity to the great mystery is a far cry from what I found when I began my training as a chaplain in the general hospital setting. Consigned to a place where success was measured by medical cure, the dying ones were hidden as if a failure and an embarrassment.

Left alone, usually at the ends of long corridors, these were the patients for whom there could be granted little time or attention, much less caring. Burdened with too many patients, too little training in psychosocial care, and no emotional support for themselves, nurses often avoided these patients for whom medical cure was impossible. This is what motivated me to go into social work. It seemed simple to me. I thought, *What do I want for me and those I love when our time to die comes?* It was not this abandonment and inhumane neglect.

So much has changed in these twenty years since I began this work. St. Christopher's in England was the first of its kind anywhere and the model and inspiration for hospice here in Branford, Connecticut. It became the first hospice in the United States and thus has been a model for many others since then. In spite of efforts to try to retain a legal right to the name to protect its unique features, the idea was ripe for the times, and the hospice concept throughout America became a movement. Almost two thousand hospices in many variations exist today. Visiting-nurse organizations include a hospice concept in the care of their patients. There are hospital-based programs for the special care of those whose prognoses require palliative care rather than cure, but as hospitals focus more on acute care, that is a very short-term option.

It is essential for you to know that whatever the

choice—it's yours to make. You are not going to be sent away to a residential hospice or a hospital or kept at home against your will. You've made thoughtful preparations already for many of the practical matters having to do with your death. You've received information from the hospitals here concerning their programs. You've been open and sensitive to the needs of your family, to those closest to you who will take care of you and surround you with love and with help. You've explored the possibilities of respite care for them—through short stays at Hartford Hospital, if you choose the services of the Visiting Nurse Association, or Connecticut Hospice, if that is your decision. I know that you would prefer, if possible, taking all possible options into consideration, to die at home. And if, as time passes, this option remains your choice—your family will support you and give you the safety, the nurturing, and the comfort that are worthy of the long physical and spiritual journey you have undertaken.

H: Of course, as I've said in this meditation, I should prefer to die at home. But I realize what a terrible burden on everyone this can (and will) be, permitting little respite from the necessity of providing continuous twenty-four-hour care and upsetting both the routine of the household and the peace and tranquility of the physical environment you have created to make this home a sanctuary. Since I, at times, have created such havoc in routine living at home, could you tolerate my dying there?

K: You do create havoc, that's true. Everyone who has lived with you knows that. Apart from that, dying at home need not be a "terrible burden," as you put it. Nurturing a loved one in comfortable and familiar surroundings can be a challenge and a gift. Yes, certain adjustments may have to be made—our dining room will have to be converted into a bedroom because we can't risk your falling on the stairs. But these changes will be temporary at best, and if they contribute to your care and comfort and to the ease of caring for you, they will be welcomed.

And isn't that the most important thing of all—for you to be comfortable in an environment of light, peace, and love so that the passage from this realm to the next is as natural and beautiful as possible? What your loved ones care most about is maintaining a high quality of life with you and for you—for all of us right up to the end. To help you accomplish that is our loving promise to you. It is no less than what you have done for others and would do for me. You are a master at care-giving.

H: Certainly, while I'm in possession of my faculties and relatively pain- and trouble-free, home would be an easier place for family and friends to visit and share with us their gifts of love and closeness. But how will you know when another option has to be called into play? Will I be able to play a part in the decision? What factors will govern? What part does pain control have in making the ultimate decision?

K: Control of pain is less a factor than it used to be. There are new palliative drugs and new ways of administering them. Pain control has become more effective than it used to be. There are substances, pumps, patches, time-release medications like the MS Contin you are taking, that can be administered at home. If you choose to die at home, the probability is that you will get your wish. According to the Visiting Nurse Association, very few of their home hospice patients need to go into the hospital at the very end. They die at home—peaceful, pain-free, in the most familiar and cherished environment. And again, I promise you, your wishes and choices will be honored.

H: From what I know about residential hospice care, it is strictly short-term, very terminal care ending in death without reprieve. As a place to die, doesn't admittance to hospice create needless anxiety and depression through the certainty that this is really it? That one will not get out alive?

K: A residential hospice is a wonderful place to die. It is available only to patients with two months or less to live—and it creates an environment in which every person, every care-giver, every service is dedicated to making the last days and weeks pain-free, stress-free, secure, and nurturing. Hospice alleviates the fear that you are not going to be taken care of, that nothing can be done. The family is considered the unit of care and is welcome at any time. There are no set visiting hours. Volunteers and professional staff are dedicated to one and only one objective—making death an experience of physical and spiritual peace for the patient, friends, and family alike. Hospice itself is beautifully designed architecturally. There are no rooms in which a dying person can be hidden away. Patients are cared for in a center atrium. There is privacy, but at the same time, openness, light, plants, bird feeders, airiness, and quiet. There is a nursery for children, a playground outside, a room for prayer and meditation. And, of course, there is a team from every relevant discipline that ministers to the physical, psychological, spiritual, and emotional needs of the patient and the family.

Hospice also provides short-term respite to a family when loved ones want to die at home. And, of course, it is not a place where you are "put," but a place where you have freely chosen to go and so must understand your medical prognosis. True, it is also a place where death inevitably takes place. But there is also the option to leave, to return home if that is what you want. I think we are very fortunate that here in Connecticut, within an hour's drive from here, we have the first specially designed hospice in the United States.

H: On the other hand, I have felt about hospitals that they do offer the possibility of getting better, of even a temporary reprieve from the death sentence. And they do not force the terrible dislocations created by trying to adapt home to the needs of a dying person. Nor is there the terrible finality that the hospice imposes, a pain-free, comfortable environment without any reprieve. What are the liabilities of choosing to die in a hospital? The two weeks I spent most recently at St. Francis Hospital seemed to prove this point. I was cared for lovingly and efficiently, but I never had the fear that I was going to die there—even when, on the night I was rushed to the emergency room, it seemed as if that might happen.

K: Hospice care doesn't allow much room for denial and it is not for everyone. You are lucky that St. Francis Hospital is such a caring place, but you were there because you needed acute care. There have been great improvements in hospital care over the past ten years or so, especially in the quality of nursing care. But the fact remains that the hospital is not the place that is centered or focused on the needs of the dying patient. So long as you, as a patient, can benefit from the services the hospital provides, you are welcome to stay there. But as soon as it is clear that you are going to die, your options are limited to being discharged to your own home or to a nursing home if you cannot be cared for where you live.

In the hospital you also run the danger of being caught up in a system in which you have no control over your dying. This is a very real danger.

H: I know there are many variations now on the original hospice concept. Yes, it takes a lot of the agonizing out of that choice. But once we've accepted a home-hospice program, how free will you and I be to create our own environment for dying and death? Should we begin right now to make plans or wait and see how things progress over time?

K: The home-hospice program offers some of the special services you need: regular visits by a nurse for medical assessment and monitoring; help with the providing of special equipment such as a hospital bed, wheelchair, etc.; twenty-four-hour availability in case of an emergency; a social worker for support for you and for your family; a volunteer assigned just to you; and a chaplain if needed. Their experience with the special needs of people who have limited prognoses is invaluable. They are able also to assist your own physician in decisions about pain control.

Because of our overreliance on the medical model of

care, we have become very dependent on others to be responsible for us. We surrender autonomy, integrity, decision making, self-reliance, and self-confidence. In other words, we give to someone else authority over ourselves. That is a big problem throughout life, and becomes more so when we are ill, aging, or dying.

We began our thinking about dying and death by considering it as a natural life process to be learned about and prepared for. The preparation begins early in life. But when we put all our reliance on a source outside of ourselves, we lose touch with our divine core and with our power. We persist in believing that modern science and technology can find and solve every health problem, and when we so often observe that this is not true, we are confused, disappointed, and angry.

Some of the so-called "alternative" approaches to health care promote a greater reliance on self-awareness and responsibility. They are more apt to recognize and utilize the natural healing properties of the mind and body. The traditional medical model has become most effective in detection after you are already diseased, and in pharmacology. We need to acknowledge its limitations in order to know how to fit it into a comprehensive health-care plan. This requires more of us than expecting "the doctor" to make us well or for a health-care system to take care of us and make our decisions for us when we are really able to do it for ourselves.

To accept admission into the home-hospice program is both comforting and disturbing. It's a relief to have the kind of support they offer when you need it. On the other hand, it's another chipping away at our defensive denial that makes us want to believe that this is not really necessary. It brings the whole thing closer to home, literally.

H: Physical pain still seems to be the most compelling factor in deciding where to die. The response of hospice leadership to the Hemlock Society's handbook on suicide and euthanasia was based largely on hospice's ability to create a pain-free environment, which makes suicide based on terminal suffering unnecessary. Are there benefits other than palliation, such as companionship and atmospherics, that hospices offer to the patients and their families?

K: I can tell you that hospice does much more than create a pain-free environment. It has benefits beyond palliation. It does offer hope, cheer, and a community of families with mutual concerns. It is cheerful and upbeat with every day spent there as normal and as optimistic as possible. But the main benefit of hospice is that death is not considered a failure. It is a natural event to be lived through in a spirit of grace. And not only does it care for the needs of its patients and their families—until the moment of death—it then helps the family process its grief, handle its bereavement, and reflect on the entire mysterious and beautiful experience.

H: How much should the place of dying and death be a concern of the patient? How important is it to let go, at some point, of decision-making and put these concerns in the hands of others? If I should defer these decisions to you, like eventually going into a residential hospice, on what would you base them? Would you want to take on this responsibility if I cannot? Have you already considered the best course of action?

K: Please, at this point, after all we've talked about, don't begin to worry about losing control. I consider that you're going to be here until you're gone. You don't have to become passive and let someone else make decisions for you. I don't like it when you seem to want to surrender power, responsibility, and control. I know you can do for yourself. All your life you've been an active, aggressive decision-maker. You've been known for your energy, your authority, your accountability. I expect you to give to yourself what, all your life, you've given to others: authority and control, the power to organize events. I don't mind changes, rearrangements, but I can't accept passivity and helplessness from you except as passing moods. I know that when your energy is low there is a temptation to cop-out. But part of your journey now is not to disappear inside of yourself—but to continue as long as you can—to be yourself and to model for yourself and for us the courage and the power you have demonstrated your whole life. If you should become compromised and unable to make decisions, then I will do it for you.

H: The night a dear friend of ours died, he was virtually alone in the hospital. A priest had visited him to deliver last rites, and you had gone to share the culminating moment with him, as we both had gone the previous night. How can assurances be given that I will not die alone whatever the hour or day? That is one of my greatest fears. Yet it would demand too much of you, children, friends, and family to maintain some sort of vigil to the end just to keep me company. What has been your experience with other deaths in this regard?

K: I don't think you have to worry about that. You won't be abandoned or left alone unless you want to be. If this is a fear, we will face it, talk about it, and work it out. If you need someone to be with you, we will arrange it.

I found it interesting that our son John's dog, Buddha, died a few minutes after you, Heidi, and I arrived to say good-bye to him. I was so touched that we were there to hold him and give him a loving, very tearful farewell. Alone before we arrived, it was as if he had waited for us to be with him before he could go. After fifteen years of faithful, loyal, and loving companionship, it was somehow fitting that he would do so. The moment of death is very special for man or beast.

Our friend who died alone in the hospital died at a time that caused the least pain and disruption for everyone. That was in character for him—being sensitive and aware of the impact of his life on others. For some reason, he could not die in the presence of his family. I think if you are aware of these decisions now—as unconscious as they may be—you will die as you want to, surrounded by loved ones, or alone in quiet and peace.

H: I would like to die peacefully, without struggle—painlessly, without machines, respirators, or artificial life supports. Where is that kind of environment most likely to be created? Home, hospital, or hospice? And how much does the place matter after all?

K: As we've discussed so often, you've made the major decisions governing machines, respirators, heroic measures, and artificial life supports. You've done all you can to ensure that you will die peacefully, painlessly, and without struggle—and I've promised you that we will do everything in our power to see that your wishes and choices are carried out. Where is that most likely to happen? Certainly at home or at hospice there is a better chance that you can die naturally. Unfortunately, in some hospitals you can't be absolutely certain that a committee or an individual doctor won't try to keep you alive if there is a possibility that you can be somehow restored—even temporarily. But the main point I want to make is that the place really doesn't matter when you've prepared for your death as responsibly as you have. Everyone, from your family to your doctor and your lawyer knows what you want: to die effortlessly, without a struggle. There will be no machines. No one is going to try to keep you alive when you are ready for death. You will be safe and protected wherever it happens.

As you have learned to live with the idea of dying, you seem to be less frantic, less insecure about what is going to happen—and where and when. You have been able to acknowledge your fears about the process and to help respond to all of our concerns. And now, just live with the control and the grace with which, someday, you will die. Meanwhile, to have created a first-floor haven for you in our dining room is only the beginning of what I hope will be a long process of meeting each other's needs, of being able to give and receive love, and of being able to sacrifice something of ourselves for each other, which is, after all, the meaning of love and, as I think we both believe, the central purpose of living.

MEDITATION 11—LETTING GO

Near the end of her life, my stepmother, Dora, retreated to a world of blankness and lay all day in a nursing-home bed, a tiny, shrunken figure against the white sheets. She recognized no one. She did not communicate. It was clear that she was ready for death, but she was unable, unconsciously, to let go. Kay thought that Dora might be afraid to give in to death, and she set out to reassure her. One day, at the nursing home, she leaned over Dora's bed and in a calm, confident voice told her she had nothing to fear; that she could let go of life; that she was safe and loved. She repeated these phrases even though there was no reaction. Suddenly, as Kay was telling her once again that there was nothing to fear, Dora opened her eyes, eyes that had the old shine and mischief. She looked up at Kay and said, "Why, Kay, how nice to see you. What a lovely dress you're wearing." She rallied from her retreat with enough vigor to live another several weeks. It was as if she were refusing to acknowledge the inevitability of death. Even with advanced age and compromised physical and mental abilities, she seemed never to have considered her own death.

Now that I know that none of the National Cancer Institute protocols have worked, and my time is limited, I must focus my attention on quality, not quantity of life. I began the Suramin protocol in no pain, with no weakness, and no symptoms. After nine weeks of Suramin, the drug has weakened my legs, killed my adrenal gland, caused edema in my feet, and peripheral neuropathy in my fingers. Because my legs have weakened, I've been given a cane and told to use it whenever I walk. My bone marrow is not producing enough hemoglobin, so I must have two units of blood transfused every couple of weeks to take the strain off my heart which, for the first time in my life, has developed a murmur. Because of the death of the adrenal gland, I have developed cataracts in both eyes and, as a final insult, when I returned from my last evaluation in August 1991, I developed a triple pneumonia that put me back in the hospital for three weeks.

The doctors have offered the option of continuing with one of three new experimental protocols, each of which is by mouth, with few side effects, and the chance of extending my life by six months to a year. Time, even measured in months, has suddenly become precious. I am greedy for it knowing that Death will inevitably end his holiday and take me through the final door.

At work, I had been fighting to remain employed until I reach seventy, a promise to me which had been made and broken. My employers wanted me to continue to meet their needs at a greatly reduced salary and no benefits. "We just don't have the money," they said.

So, like Dora lying in a fetal position at the bottom of her crib, I must let the idea of "letting go" penetrate my defenses and bring me to a place where I can no longer be defined by my work, my energy, my ability, my pride, my ego. I must let go of the phantoms of service, of accomplishment, and of self-importance that have pursued me for almost fifty years.

What will I do? Will I jeopardize what life remains by letting go of the purposes and energies which gave such meaning to my life? So many men, when they have let go voluntarily or been let go from a life of work, curl up and perish within months of their retirement. Even with new hormonal protocols, will death come more quickly than the time for which the cancer has me scheduled, because I have lost so many of what have seemed indispensable purposes of my life?

If I do let go and put myself into my own hands; if I do let go of job and career, of the pursuit of justice over promises made and broken; if I do let go and admit that I am dying and graciously let death come, am I violating some fundamental law of "fight, rally, don't give in to death and dying"? Am I caving in to fate and refusing, in the words of Dylan Thomas, to "rage, rage against the dying of the light"? Am I betraying the call of Tennyson's "Ulysses," which has been the motto of my life, "To strive, to seek, to find, and not to yield"? In the poem "Reluctance," Robert Frost wrote:

> . . . Ah, to the heart of man, was it ever less than a treason
> To go with the drift of things, to yield with a grace to reason,
> And bow and accept the end of a love or a season?

If I let go now, is it a treason? I must ask Kay.

CONVERSATION 11—LETTING GO

HERB: When I first meditated on this theme in late spring 1991, I was still working, still filling my life with the activities that seemed so essential to defining it and giving it meaning. And then, when I recognized that the experimental protocol had not halted the advance of the disease, I just stopped.

What changes have you noticed since I "let go" so precipitously? Has letting go of job and usefulness transformed me from being active in the face of life to passivity in the face of death? Doesn't "letting go" imply a surrender to the inevitable?

KAY: I had been very worried about your leaving your job. In the past, whenever we tried to discuss any alternative to your working in Washington, you were very defensive, even going so far as to accuse me of trying to destroy you. You would become wild. It was clear that your identity was enmeshed with your job. I can't even say it was your work, because you had other work. It was that job. It meant everything to you.

The sacrifices we had to make were enormous. In the beginning, when you were away one night a week, I could manage, even enjoy, a little separation. But, there was the usual extra time away from home, on business trips, "redeyes" from here to there. Then, in 1984, you started working three days a week in Washington, which meant that you were gone three nights a week. Even that wasn't so bad because I, too, was working those evenings.

One day, I realized that I was the only member of the family in Connecticut during the week. I felt abandoned. But the most difficult part was trying to adapt to the constantly changing pace—which was very quiet without you and very hectic and chaotic with you. You, the only child, demand all of my attention when you are home and get it.

I've always had conflicted feelings about wanting you here and being relieved when you weren't.

I guess what I longed for was something more evenly paced, more "normal." I wanted to take ballroom dancing and German lessons with you and go to the movies during the week. We are such good companions and have so much fun together. I wanted to be able to create a social life with you here in Hartford, but you wanted to keep on the go and to have me to yourself alone. It was my impression that you needed to be in two places or somewhere in between. Staying home in Hartford wasn't enough for you, and I understand that, too.

You've left me somewhat breathless and overwhelmed. I always said that I didn't want to be the one to have to pick up the pieces when everyone in Washington was done with you. I sensed that that would happen, that you would be let go before you were ready to let go on your own. There was no flexibility in you about creating a different life-style in these years beyond sixty-five. I don't believe in retirement. I don't really know what retirement means. I believe that work is a necessary part of life. And now, since you've had to stop going to Washington, I regret deeply that no options are left for us. I knew the only way you would stop is if you were forced to, and that is what has happened.

I was concerned that you would die as soon as you left your job. There have been a few times when you seemed lethargic and depressed, times when the cancer is all you've talked about and thought about. The stress of leaving your job and the stress about the way it happened have had a serious effect on you. I've felt that I've had to emphasize and reinforce the idea that you still have a great contribution to make in this world, apart from the work with the Kennedy Foundation. Identification with your work has been very destructive. You say "letting go of job and usefulness" as if they were synonymous. You seemed to think that letting go of job and letting go of life were the same thing. Now, when we crave precious time together, the choice is not left to us. At this time, a couple of uncluttered hours free of the "one more thing that needs to be done"—or hours free of pain or with enough energy—are spent trying to make a literal deadline of finishing this book. But it is so enjoyable, rewarding, and satisfying to be working with you, I don't want it to end.

"Letting go" may mean giving yourself permission to make changes. It may also refer to the natural withdrawal that occurs as you approach death. And, it may mean surrendering to death with acceptance.

H: Obviously, I have "let go," because either consciously or unconsciously, I no longer have the will or the strength to keep going as I was before. But letting go has not been the traumatic experience I thought it would be. I don't have a sense of struggling to maintain some status in the world of affairs. Nor do I feel that if I do let go, I'll drop into a black hole. I do have a sense of dropping into an unfamiliar but comfortable world of reflection, quiet, and rediscovery. Yet you have criticized me, I think, for not being more vigorous in a pursuit of meaning and purpose that would take the place of what I left behind. Can letting go be conditional? What would you have me do now so that "letting go" does not mean giving up?

K: It is necessary to remember that you and I will be in different places with this business of letting go. I am not a disinterested bystander. You are my husband and your letting go means that I will lose you to death. Unless you die suddenly, I know we will be ready together, but this may not be the way it is in the meantime.

This is really difficult to respond to, because a part of me still believes you are not going to die, and the denial makes the time bearable for me. But it is also hard to acknowledge that you can't keep up the breakneck pace that you had before. In the beginning, when I thought of "letting go," I thought of the job, a kind of letting go that is really preparation for change. But I find that the language you use associates your death with the ending of your work, and my thoughts about that remind me of what happened when our dear pet Bee Cat was dying.

We had gotten a new kitten, "Betty Friedan." She came into our lives and our home as another pet, Bee Cat, sat in a chair in the sunroom, unable to move. Her body was already growing cold, and it was clear that she was very near death. All of us, sitting with her, sensed that something mysterious, fearful, and beautiful was happening. The kitten came into the room and suddenly jumped up on the chair where Bee was resting. She sniffed and started to box the dying cat's head, trying to get some reaction. The attempt of the kitten to rouse Bee to life was very moving, but Bee's inability to respond confirmed that she was on the brink of death.

Sometimes I feel the same way now about you. Letting go of you is very hard. When you are sitting lethargically in your chair, I want to stir a response in you; to pick a fight, to jump up on the chair and box your ears. It feels so good when you do respond, and I feel it's no coincidence that this conversation, though not the last, is the last to be written;

the one we've been putting off for weeks. I am obviously having a hard time letting go. Some days part of me feels that the longer we keep writing, the longer you will keep going. And I want to keep you going, because I feel that the longer your life has meaning and purpose, the longer life will matter to you.

I don't want you to give up. Your passivity bothers me in a number of ways. You gave at the office, as I've said before, and now you often seem to lack the energy or the will to keep going here at home. While I don't want you to let go before our work together is done, I can't forget that you never, never let the Foundation down—even after they were abandoning you. So I keep the pressure on. And I don't like that either.

H: With the expectation of a few months of life, I'm aware that everything—from the turning of the seasons, to holidays, birthdays, and special occasions, is probably for me, a last-time experience. This makes everything more pregnant with meaning. Yet it also fosters the awareness that, one page at a time, I am letting go of life itself. To know that this is the last Thanksgiving, the last Christmas, the last novels by Anne Tyler or Robertson Davies, the last trip on a plane, is both depressing and strangely seductive. Since this awareness heightens the real and symbolic significance of every such experience, should I be closing doors, one by one, bowing to those who have set my sentence? If I pretend that everything is normal and, of course, will be repeated in the next cycle of seasons and occasions, does this not rob me of the chance to extract every ounce of sweetness from these experiences—knowing they will not be repeated?

K: On my birthday a few days ago, you gave me a beautiful bracelet with a card that said that this would not be the last present. Our daughter Heidi remarked how many last trips and last presents we've had over the past three years. We've often laughed about how we've milked these three years of last things. They gave us the excuse to do some of the things we wanted to do—and so we did them. I have a strong sense of unreality that it is all going to end. It's very subtle. Even though the knowledge of their finality has let us savor many of these "last things," it's hard for me to believe they won't happen again. There is such sadness and disbelief that I can't say I've actually "savored" any of them. I can't truly enjoy them when I'm so aware that this or that may never again be ours to share. It's a contradiction. How can you and I face the awareness that every day, perhaps, we are doing something for the last time? I can understand how this perception gives you a greater appreciation of nature—the sky, the leaves, the gardens; and I know that brings you both joy and sadness, wonder and tears. But the price of constant awareness of the ending of life is a great deal of stress and ambivalence. There is always a double meaning—a double message. On the one hand, this savoring of experience seems like the heart and core of living life, rather than just existing in life; on the other hand, it is a denial of life that could have flowered for you for many years to come. Sometimes I wonder if I'm not bargaining—and the bargain is that if we face this head-on and not let go, we shall be spared the loss.

H: If I let go of things that in the past seemed so essential to my life, there is an undeniable void, a depression that cannot be life-enhancing. Yet, if I simply create another busy agenda to take its place, am I not defeating the whole purpose of letting go—the creation of a very special place and time to review, share, and learn from the unique process I am going through? Is this not the best use of this time of dying unto death?

K: I will not allow you to create another busy agenda just to fill time. And, again, this may be another kind of bargaining on my part. As long as you are doing important work you will stay alive longer. So what I am saying—for me—is that I'm perfectly willing to have you let go of things that are not essential for your well-being. but I'm very disturbed when you seem to want to let go of things I think are important to life itself. I just can't face that.

H: I understand what you are saying. The day I learned that there was little or no hope of slowing down the march of the cancer medically, my 1991 calendar and appointment book dropped and fell apart. As I tried to reassemble the pages, and as I reviewed the constant activity that characterized my days until now, I realized with much pain and guilt how trivial most of this activity was. The writing of this book is an essential part of "letting go," so that I can fully experience this new stage of my life and make reparation to you for my failure to put first things first—before they became "last things." How can I find other forms of mental or spiritual activity, other strategies for making this time a richer, more productive experience?

K: Just live life as it comes every day. I don't know if it needs to be productive. I think about the question in terms of letting go of the things that you don't want to do. You are the only one who can decide what those are. There are some things we sometimes need to do which don't have great significance and are not very earth-shaking. My women friends and I talk a lot about our clothes and hair, and it might sound to someone else as if we think these things are the very essence of life. The other night we spent the whole evening being very silly. It was important to take a break from all the seriousness and sorrow of the world.

The other part is that time is very precious. It's important to eliminate those things that don't suit your purposes right now. Your resources are too limited to spend them on assignments and requests to work from those who have relied on your talents for so long. One of the advantages of coming to terms with dying and death is that you can then forget about it, and enjoy the new freedom and appreciation it gives you to live your life any way you want to.

As to letting go of life itself, it's letting go of things that no longer matter. You have noticed that you care less and less about the latest financial scandals, political gossip, and transitory events of the world. Even during the Senate hearings on Clarence Thomas, and the Willy Smith trial, you couldn't bear to watch, while I was almost obsessed by them. Now you are less interested in the transitory, and more interested in pursuing ideas and things of the spirit.

H: I sense the danger of letting go of people as well as of business as usual. That's why I've called so many old friends—some not revisited for forty or fifty years, to ask them to have lunch, to get together, to share our lives and thoughts. I sometimes feel that I am imposing the sad fate of a dying man on friends who are in the bloom of health. Yet, if I don't make the first move, I'm afraid that none will be made toward me. How can I handle this personal outreach so that I am neither asking others to share my burden nor imposing on them the last wishes of a dying friend?

K: Handle it the way you feel like handling it. The outreach you've already done has met with gratifying results. Your reunion with a large group of your high school friends—Class of 1939—meant so much to you, you are still talking about it. And when one of your classmates came all the way to Hartford when you were in the hospital, you were deeply moved. Yesterday, someone you did not want to see came to the door, someone you find it very difficult to be with. You made it clear that this was not the time for a visit, whereas before now, you would have invited him in because your image of yourself was "Mr. Please Everyone." As life narrows down, the circle of people in your life narrows down, too. As the beautiful *September Song* says so poignantly—"The days dwindle down to a precious few . . . and these few precious days I'll spend with you, these precious days I'll spend with you." So this is a question that almost answers itself, for me as well as for you.

H: If I hadn't become involved in the Suramin protocol, I might still be physically vigorous and devoid of those debilitating side effects which have so weakened me. After the Suramin failed, the doctors at the National Cancer Institute told me that if we didn't try to "cap" or slow down the escalation of the prostate specific antigens, the quality of my life would disintegrate rapidly in a sea of pain. So I tried two more experiments at home—pills by mouth—and they have failed me, too. Palliative radiation has checked the pain, but I know that inside my bones the cancer is rushing toward a climax. How, in the light of these situations, will I know when to give up? How will I know when even the option of letting go is being taken from me?

K: We always want answers from outside ourselves. This is one that is totally within you. You will know. An inner voice, sometimes referred to a spiritual guide, has spoken to you in your dreams and meditations. That is where you will find the answers to your questions. Every month, every week, every day, every minute, you will experience the course of your journey before you die. You will not be letting go of life until you stop breathing. You will be ready for it when it happens. You will know when the time has come to let go—completely—peacefully, safely.

Your anxiety seems to come about because of your fear that you will be taken from us before you are ready to go. So you might say that you are holding on to finish this project, which has given you such a strong grasp on life. You once sang a song to me about a young man whose sweetheart was as ill as you are now. The doctors, in the summer, had told him that when the leaves fell from the trees, his lover would die. And so he was "tying the leaves to the trees so my sweetheart will not die." We are not tying leaves to trees, but neither are we content to sit idly by and watch the leaves fall. We've been given some leeway, and we're taking it.

H: I keep coming back to the fact that the Suramin imposed weakness and fatigue, coupled now, in March, with palliative radiation and the thrice-daily morphine, producing a lassitude that makes any thought of "affirmative action" seem, at times, overwhelming. Isn't my body telling me something about letting go?

K: Maybe it's that you just need to conserve your energy right now. My sense of it is that sometimes you are experiencing weakness from Suramin, sometimes fatigue from radiation, and sometimes depression. It's hard to tell the difference between depression and despair and fatigue. You certainly have reason for all these feelings once in a while. And, they are largely unfamiliar to you.

H: I've read that cancer patients are supposed to fight, and not give in to predictions or prophecies having to do with life span. Yet, by fighting for a marginally extended time of life, am I not denying that the experience of dying and death may have even greater value and meaning than holding on to a few more weeks or even months? At what point is "letting go" an invitation to death to come and take me? By holding on so fast to life here on this plane, am I not expressing an unnatural resistance to what my body, mind, and spirit are telling me? Should I be a "fighter" and risk being regarded as a failure if I don't extend my life or produce a remission, or even a cure?

K: Regardless of what has been said and written, no one but you is the expert about your death. There are no experts outside ourselves. The only thing I can say is that we live our dying and death in a way that is consistent with the way we live life. Thus far, you're living this experience in an appropriate and consistent way for you, and I believe that being judgmental about this or communicating an unrealistic denial of death is facile and arrogant. The only way it could have been different is if you were an entirely different person. We've sensed this from the beginning. It hurt me that this is true, but I've had to accept your handling of your living, dying, and death in your own way.

Through this long year of conversations, I've tried to respond to your questions, help you resolve your doubts, ease your fears. Now I believe with all my heart that you are ready to face death with your customary courage and grace. You expect no miracles but have a clear-eyed vision of a life that does not end at the garden gate, but promises an eternity beyond. And I hope, from whatever realm, you will tell me that I'm right.

MEDITATION 12—COMING HOME

It is early October 1991. I sit in a reclining chair at St. Francis Hospital in Hartford, receiving two units of whole blood to boost my hemoglobin count, which has fallen below the desired level. If I focus my inner vision on the marrow of my bones, I can almost see the tumors jostling and crowding out the tiny factories that produce the life-giving red blood cells.

Seated around me are men and women receiving blood or chemo or other intravenous therapies. I am the stranger. To one another, they are old friends. One woman has been coming here for a transfusion every week for thirteen years.

You would think they were sitting around the Laundromat waiting for the dryer to complete its cycle. While the fluid drips into their veins, they swap stories about children, grandchildren, husbands. They exchange gossip about celebrities. They talk candidly about the progress of their disease, as if that were part of the small talk of every group of middle-aged men and women.

In all that company, there is no apparent realization that in many ways they are extraordinary, unusually brave, stoic, optimistic, resolved. They know they have limited life expectancies, limited strength, limited choices. But their cheerfulness and sociability seem to wipe out, temporarily at least, the stress of living with metastatic disease.

As I sit there, the stranger in their midst, I feel that I am, at the same time, both an observer and one of their fellowship. Because of my own very guarded prognosis, I can empathize with their fears, their victories, and their determination to live out each day until the days, at last, run out.

The bright fall sky lends brilliance and poignancy to the day. Here in Connecticut, the leaves are turning slowly. The trees along the streets and against the hillside are still mostly green with occasional flares of gold, orange, and crimson. Last weekend, in Vermont, the foliage was its gaudy, giddy brightest; some trees so perfect in their autumn dress that it took your breath away to see them standing like torches against the blue October sky.

According to my medical advisors, this will be my last fall, last Halloween, last Thanksgiving, last snow, last Christmas. I carry that knowledge with me like the dull ache of a toothache blunted by analgesics. With the advent of 1992, I will have reached the mid-point of my seventieth year. I stretch eagerly toward my birthday in July; to reach it is one of my fondest hopes. My father died five months after his allotted three score and ten. But he had been suffering heart pain and anxiety for eight years, while I, until the "Suramin cure" devastated my body, was enjoying exceptional health and vigor.

It would be cheap bathos to concentrate on "last things," to clutch to an aching heart, each month's never-to-be-repeated treasures, to try to hold tightly, miserly, to each precious golden coin of the seasons, rather than spend them freely and exuberantly.

Thanks to our "Conversations at Midnight," whispered in intimacy when we were together, or taking the form of telephone calls and written dialogue during the weeks we were apart, I have changed in strange and unexpected ways since our dialogue began. My fears of dying and death have been resolved. My feelings of loss and bereavement have been almost neutralized by a sense of joy and wonder in the knowledge that I am not moving toward oblivion but, rather, that I am "coming home." I am not even sure I know what "coming home" means. But I am certain in my deepest being, that I have begun a new and unexpectedly exciting and beautiful part of the journey back to the source, to the mystery from which I emerged into this life seventy years ago.

Gone is the terror that my unique, individual consciousness may come to an end; gone is the egocentric need to affirm the continuity of myself. I seem to live now surrounded by a ring of light whose source I cannot decipher. The poignancy of pumpkins, of fall foliage, of holidays, of music and poetry are still precious, but no longer the indispensable furniture of home.

Home is no longer earthbound, anchored by gravity, measured by days and years. Home is the garden dreamed of by the God of my dream. And as the growing assault on my body propels me toward that doorway called death, I feel that my spirit has broken free. And whether the garden on the other side of the door is filled with flowers or light, or nothing at all, it is home. And you, Kay, have given me the strength and the wisdom to find it and to be content.

And yet, and yet, our literal home here on Westland Avenue has never seemed sweeter—and never have I been so reluctant to leave this for the eternal home that lies so close to me now. Is this a typical reaction, a common experience of longing for life and fear of the unknown? Is it a sign that I am not yet ready to exchange my earthly home for eternity? I must ask Kay.

CONVERSATION 12—COMING HOME

HERB: When I wrote the words *Coming Home* as the subject of our final conversation, I didn't really know what I meant. I was still the skeptic, the realist, the man who was convinced that death was the end of all being, all consciousness, and while that terrified and saddened me, I was resigned to the fact that that's the way it is. Period. The end. What was there about death that could possibly signify a homecoming? But then, over this past year, I have become increasingly comfortable with the idea, the knowledge that death is only a portal to an eternity that has both mystery and meaning. I have become convinced that although, on this side of the door, I cannot penetrate the mystery, it will be unfolded for me—for all of us—when we reach the other side. So now, after you have guided me so lovingly to a more spiritual perception of the universe and my place in it, I am able to say without embarrassment that whatever "coming home" means, my death will speed me there, from this temporal home to a home with the larger, infinite mystery.

And yet, and yet, I find myself more reluctant than ever to leave this beautiful home in this world. I find myself torn between anticipation of the home that lies before me, behind the door to the garden, and this home you have made for me to live and die in.

Of course, I have been fortunate—almost inexplicably so—in remaining mostly pain-free during this part of the journey. Not that the disease and the various unsuccessful protocols haven't taken their toll, but without pain, or erupting tumors, or the interruption of any vital function, especially intellectual activity, I am unable to locate the cancer as the cause of my dying. And so, while I am resolved about my death, death in the spring, as every doctor has predicted, I want to extend, as far as possible, my time on this side of the door. And I want to make the best use of this time while I am still able. Is my clinging to this home, somehow a lingering doubt, or denial that the eternal home you have so convinced me of is not after all real?

KAY: I am surprised by my own capacity for denial. I feel that even though we've been talking about death so intensely and writing this book about it, somehow preparing for death seems like a celebration, a big event for which we are getting ready. I'm saddened when I remember that we are moving toward a celebration of a sort in which you will not be with us. This is my experience of the same thing you are talking about. There is something so wonderful happening. But it is something full of loss and sadness for me. I'm still feeling mostly a great sense of unreality—so much so because you have such a strong personality with such powerful mental energy. Despite the insults to your body, the exploding prostate specific antigens, the daily dosage of morphine, you are as energetic and lively as ever. And so again, we sit here and talk and read and sing, and it seems that nothing's wrong. How could anything be wrong with the place where we are now? I hope you are not evaluating your behavior judgmentally, but are just observing what is happening within you when fear of death is gone, when there is even a sense of excitement about this ultimate homecoming, as you call it, and that this is balanced by a strengthening desire to hold on as long as possible to your home here with me.

Are you saying that you are too content and happy to be thinking about dying and are finding it hard to accept death, now that you've resolved your fears and doubts? As someone said to us the other day, who wouldn't be happy and contented in the place you are now, your hospice at home. Here, you are surrounded by caring people, your dog and cat are by your side; there are flowers, beautiful music, and, best of all, for you, you are the center of everyone's attention. You even have the telephone, by which you've lived your life, at your side. In addition, you have the satisfaction of giving your attention to some of the things about which you've been procrastinating or avoiding altogether. I think of the phrase, "Live every day as if it were your last."

You are getting ready for that. You've said that you work best under a deadline. Working on our book even gives you this. So it's only half in jest that we can say, "Herb, you're a lucky guy."

What I am surprised by is how calm and collected I am most of the time. There are moments during which it feels like a nightmare. A kind of quiet comes upon me when I'm out running errands or shopping. This is my hometown. I don't think I look particularly different when I'm out in public. One is not accustomed to being outgoing and gregarious here in New England, particularly in winter. Here, dour Yankee behavior is the rule, so no one would ever know the terrible thing that is happening to me, to us. When I'm out with my daughters or a friend, we can have a good time, be lively and animated. Much of the time we appear to be having a better time than most people. And then, it comes crashing in and overwhelms me, and I want to cry out, "My husband is dying. I am dying. We are all dying."

Now, for you, there has been a kind of liberation. We've made the decision that you will not return to a hospital. Here at home you have been liberated from the rigors of the environment. You will no longer go upstairs because of our fear that you will fall and your fragile bones will collapse. So we have created for you a place of sunshine and flowers and comfort downstairs.

It was almost unbearably sad on our last night together in the bed we've shared for eleven and a half years. We were awake, conversing at midnight as we have for so many nights and early mornings. At four A.M. we were laughing and playing our game of analyzing our dreams, usually mine, the game of Herr Dr. Freud and, as usual, if we don't care for his analysis, Herr Dr. Jung. And, as we talked and laughed, I had an overwhelming sense of "last things."

You said to me once, "Do you ever recall the last time you did something that is no longer possible to do, like climb a favorite tree that's been cut down, or play with your favorite doll? How strange it would be if we knew we were doing something for the last time at the time we were doing it."

The "last times" of so many things have already occurred for us. I awakened recently crying because I realized you would never read another book to me. You've read dozens of books aloud during our marriage—at night when I couldn't sleep, as we floated lazily down the Rhine, for hours in cafés in Austria while I knitted, and during rests along hiking trails in Switzerland. I know I am the only sighted woman alive who has had the whole of Thomas Mann's *The Magic Mountain* read aloud to her. I am probably the only one, too, to have had the subtitles of the Japanese movie *A Taxing Woman* and the three-hour-long Danish film *Pelle the Conqueror* read aloud from start to finish even at times when she was asleep during the video screenings. We are mercifully spared the knowledge of so many "last things." Our last night together in our bed is one that is unbearable to linger on.

H: We began this conversation in mid-October sitting on a sun-drenched patio in Santa Fe during the ten-day trip that we thought would probably be our last away from home. I felt so keenly that Taos and Santa Fe had a peace and beauty that reinforced my desire and my will not to leave this earth too soon. I find that great beauty and our companionship move me constantly between the twin poles of tears and laughter. Yet, as I've said, I know these experiences are part of the home I am inevitably leaving behind. Have I been reacting to this part of the journey differently from others we have taken together? Even though something more glorious lies ahead for me, I can't accept the passivity of just sitting and writing. A voice keeps repeating, "Not yet. Not yet." What am I waiting for? Do I still hope for a remission, a cure so I won't have to leave?

K: Even though I have imperfect use of it, I know that we have inborn knowledge of when the time to die is near. You didn't have it then, and you don't have it now in spite of the fact that your limitations are becoming painfully progressive. All during October, I somehow had the feeling that you were going to die before the end of that month. But your sense of the time left to you was more accurate. Even now, when the doctors tell us that spring is probably the outside time of survival, something within you is saying, "Not yet." This is the voice I trust most, not that of the experts. Yet we both had the definite feeling that this was our last trip, and that seems accurate. The beauty and joy we experienced were tinged with both sadness and hope—sadness at the ending of those journeys which have given us such delight; hope that the voice that says, "Not yet" will wait longer to say, "Now." Unconsciously, you knew you were not going to die when I feared you would. I was worried about the month of October because you had spoken so often of the need to be finished with the book in October. I thought that sense of a deadline was an expression of your inner awareness of the time of your death. I am grateful, as you are, that four months have passed; the book will be finished in February and you are still very much a part of our lives and our home.

H: One of the great ambiguities of the long process of dying is one's relationship with family and friends. One part of you is eager to join them, to participate actively in their lives, to be as "normal" as possible. And yet in their minds as in yours is the sure knowledge—the sixth sense—of how far you have traveled along a road that has diverged from theirs. Is this feeling of separation a natural one? Is it healthy? Should I try harder to explain how I feel and where I am or live now as if these last days were more like, than unlike, all other days?

K: This seems like a deceptively simple question. I suppose what you are wondering is—"How do I reconcile my inner need to make smaller the circle, and in doing that, how do I share this with others?" I sometimes wonder what it's like for people to be with us when we are so frank with one another, even to being careless of their sensibilities. And I wonder how our openness comes across. This is no problem for our most intimate friends; they want to share this with us. But it is a difficult question when illness and treatment have occupied so much of your attention. I've been thinking recently that some people are not able to accompany us on our journey. I realize that it is very painful for them to get in touch with their own fears that this may happen to them some day. You proudly show them your sunny, flower-filled downstairs bedroom that has so changed the character of our home. They see only a deathbed, and instead of responding empathetically to you, they shudder at their own forebodings. Some people have eliminated themselves from the circle of our friendship. Some, more firmly entrenched, only escape when we do. Some are just there, passive, at the edge of the circle. They care, but I sense that some don't want to get involved in intimacy because it is too frightening. And when you speak of death as a coming home, they think you've become compromised mentally.

Once in a while, as in some places in these midnight conversations, we seem to step out a bit too far. Then it is obvious, and we pull back. Those who can't stand it don't even bother with us. You accommodate yourself with your company, your children, all who find it hard to talk about it with you. So I've seen you respect people's distance. Right now, your condition is so fragile that you can't expend your energy on denial, covering up, and being Pollyanna. When you try to do your "I'm fine" act, you get into trouble. When you try your "whistle past the graveyard" shtick, you get into difficulties with others. Just looking at you—your loss of mobility, of weight, of hair—makes some people anxious and afraid. The only time I've seen you anxious is when you're holding back. So openness with me is essential. As you move between the home you now occupy and the home that will be yours after death, you have to understand that the rules of the house prevail; and for most of your friends and acquaintances, that means being sensitive to their fears and their sadness at the prospect of losing you.

H: I worry that at some point my road will diverge from yours as well. I still have the tendency to say "I'm fine" in answer to your questioning, whether I'm in pain or discomfort or sad or depressed. It's just that darker moods are not characteristic of the way I feel most of the time. At three o'clock yesterday morning, I found myself singing along with Martha Tilton—"I let a song go out of my heart . . ."—one of my Duke Ellington favorites. You were awakened and came downstairs to see what was wrong and remained with me for more than an hour. And I realized that my singing so loudly was less out of happiness than loneliness. I hoped you would hear and respond to my call. Would you rather know of each dip in the road or accept the fact that right now my "I *am* fine" helps keep me from becoming just another dying patient and casting gloom and despair over our beautiful home to which I have now come to stay.

K: Can you tell me specifically what you are afraid of?

H: I'm afraid I'll be a drag if I let you know of every alteration in the weather of my body and soul, every ache, weakness, and setback. Before I awakened you when I was suffering such agonizing chest pains on New Year's morning, I waited long after I should have to ask you to call the doctor. Why? I did not want to disturb the early morning tranquility of the slumbering house. Sometimes when I inadvertently groan or indicate pain aloud, I'm afraid you will think I am weak, and I often cover up by saying, "That wasn't a groan. It was just a sigh." And as my situation worsens, as it will, I'm afraid of being an unpleasant, depressing presence, as if I were ungrateful for all the support, the beauty, and the peace you have given me.

K: I'm not so sure you can keep anything from me at this point. We seem, because of our closeness born of these intimate conversations, to be almost unnaturally sensitive to each other's thoughts and words. I have a keen intuitive sense of what you are thinking and feeling—it's almost like ESP and it sometimes frightens me. It's too late now for games. And in terms of how you want to live your life in this home, before you pass through the door—that's up to you. You remember our friend Ellen, whose husband had cancer a few years ago. He never complained once, she told me. He never revealed to her, talked to her about his pain, his sorrow, but kept it all inside. For them, that worked. He needed to be stoic; she needed to be protected. I always feel better when things are out in the open. With my strong, intuitive sense, mixed signals, denial, drive me crazy. To the contrary, I don't find the truth destructive at all. I find it comforting, because it affirms something I may already know at some level. And so, if you want to tell me, I'd rather know. But if you want to hide it because it does something important for you, then just do it. When you get in trouble—and you can't really put it off—that's when things get in a tangle.

H: It strikes me as somewhat odd that throughout these past two years the consolations of traditional religion have seemed totally alien to me. I have "created" a God who created the universe because "He" dreamed of a garden. That God, that garden, and that source have given me the greatest comfort of my life—a sense of "home" that I never felt before. These images seem my own—like the image of the angel I have not only seen but felt—but they must be shared by others. Have you come upon these "dying" images before? Are they only my own personal vision and imagery or do they come from a collective unconscious common to all?

K: Every person is unique, though I am sure there are many common features in our imagery of dying and death—both conscious and unconscious. I've never spent as much time talking about these subjects as with you. Sometimes, with clients or patients, time is so short and the problems of their lives right now are so compelling. What seems to be common, though, is a sense of a beautiful, safe place among people who know you and love you. I believe we must have some of these images in our "collective unconscious," and that's why I want to explore Jungian psychology, to become more familiar with the common, archetypical images we have. That's why Joseph Campbell is so appealing. Cross-cultural mythology demonstrates the prevalence of common themes, myths, and prayers. And I find in the little Jungian work I have done that the richness of studying symbols can really help our understanding of the questions you are raising out of your unique experience.

When I began to study theology at Trinity College in the 1970s, I studied the nature and knowledge of God from many perspectives. I went on to explore Death of God Theology and Process Theology. I discovered that the symbols and myths that had once guided me no longer carried meaning. In this time between myths, with the death of the patriarchal father God, we are having to search for and discover our own God by finding and creating our own myths and symbols. This is what you are doing. The conventional imagery of heaven no longer has the power to move you. It doesn't feel like home to you. Even when you see a creature with wings, the figure is one of mystery, not the familiar harp-playing seraphim or cherubim. We are living in a difficult, transitional time, but I have been inspired by others who are exploring this new ground. I have been especially moved by the group of psychiatrists, psychologists, social workers, theologians, and other therapists who are willing to explore spirituality and psychotherapy, science and true religion. This has strengthened my own conviction and helped you reconcile your doubt and longing. These mentors are really just people who acknowledge the need for spiritual development and growth and find that these don't have to be separate from their intellectual disciplines and relegated to another compartment consisting of images and rituals displayed only at certain times of the week.

The most inspiring and beautiful people I've known in the last few years are those who are taking seriously the issue of psychotherapy and spirituality, like our friend Tomas Agosin, whose sudden death has left me and many more, I know, with such a deep sense of personal loss. Here was a man who combined a keen intellect and eager curiosity with the courage to explore the interface between psychotherapy and spirituality, and as a person, he was able to show warmth, compassion, and humility.

I know that your experience studying with Tomas and his team of psychotherapists gave you confidence in the validity of what you and I have been talking through in these conversations. It is no accident, I believe, that so many truly wise and beautiful people have come into your life during these past three years as sources of inspiration and consolation. They have, in this transitional time, when the old images no longer have the power to move you, when the spiritual home, stripped of its traditional furniture, can be very lonely and bleak, suggested new images and new paths to the spiritual home that we carry within us and that never fails. they have taken very seriously, as I have, your image of a God who created the universe because he dreamed of a garden. For even though this theme—the image of an Eden—is common to so many religions—you have made it your own. You see it not as part of a mythology of creation but a beautiful reality that lies beyond the door that, at death, opens between this home and the next. And so, for you, the culminating metaphor is not the choice between a long sleep and the chance to talk with Homer, but one of love, the garden beyond the gate, the eternal, mysterious Eden of your dream of the dreaming God.

When I was in Taos last spring without you, I found a painting of geese entering a garden through a blue gate in an adobe wall. I wanted to buy it for you but, when I returned to do so, the gallery was closed, and we had to leave for our return to Santa Fe. This fall, when you and I were there together, we found the painting waiting for us in the back room of the gallery, safe from the threat of purchase by anyone else. And now it hangs in your bedroom sanctuary, a fitting image of what you are expressing at some deep level. It contains not only the metaphor of the garden but the garden gate as well, suggestive of the journey—to which you refer so often—that is taking you from one home to another through the garden gate. And just as you've been able to keep your perspective and humor throughout the journey, the waddling geese remind us that the passage to death and beyond is not gloomy, but an adventure into the unknown that is familiar, scary, and exciting at the same time. Instead of waiting for death to come to you, you perceive it as your own active journey, of coming home rather than a passive standing-by for the door to open. This gives you a sense of control, and you can experience the challenge of growing, becoming, still moving toward the light. So what you have is not only an ultimate destination, but a place now to rest and grow. A home.

H: The awareness of "last things" makes them seem more precious and poignant, but their loss does not seem to bring as much grief as I thought it would. I do want to hold on to what I have, whom and what I love—but I realize that I must be willing to "let go" before I can truly "come home" through the portal of death. I know this seems self-centered, even cold, but it seems to be part of a natural process that is beyond reason or control. What is your feeling now that our roads are beginning to diverge?

K: How can I respond beyond just saying that you must continue on your path wherever it leads? But even as you ask the question, I must say that it is not that way for me right now. I'm conscious that this is your dying, not mine, so I'm not ready to "let go" of anything more just yet, of life, of you. I feel so strongly that this is not where I am. I feel the widening gulf of separation between us and painfully realize that you are dying, and I am not. Doesn't this seem strange? There is a part of me that wants to say, "What do you mean, letting go or giving up? How can you let go of all this? How can you let go of me so easily?" I've probably tried to seduce you into staying longer by creating a beautiful place in which to die, by adding assignments and chapters to this book. And yet I know that this year of preparation and conversation has led to this. As your partner in these dialogues, I am pleased that you have come this far toward acceptance and understanding. As your wife, I am grief-stricken. I guess one final thing I want to say is how hard it is for me to be philosophical when I am immersed in my own grief. At times everything, all comfort, seems to fly out the window leaving me broken and despairing. How can it be any other way?

I remember thinking these words when I decided to marry you, realizing that the fourteen-year difference in our ages would catch up with us soon: "'Tis better to have loved and lost than never to have loved at all." I knew I was taking the chance of losing you too soon, that we would not be walking into the sunset together. It's like the disparity between our life span and that of our pets, our cats and dogs. It's always seemed so cruel.

We are doing this—as we have done everything else—together, with considerable intellectual resources and emotional stamina. As we did with my father's care, we've put everything into it, and what we have drawn from it is a wealth of riches and intimacy. And that may be part of the difficulty there is between recognizing what is going to happen and our denial that it must happen. Every bit of us is in it. I can't do it any other way. But I have a sense that if I just put my whole self into it, I will bring my whole self through it and out of it. And even as we have nurtured and strengthened you for your coming home, I, too, have been strengthened for my own. I love you.

Chapter Four

GUIDED IMAGERY

THE POWER OF THE IMAGINATION

THE CAVE EXERCISE MENTIONED IN CONVERSATION 9 was my first venture into the realm of guided imagery. I was genuinely surprised to find a message already written on an imaginary wall that I had not consciously put there. It revealed an inner resource I had not known was there. The message spoke directly to my need and brought comfort during a time of aloneness and left me with the knowledge that there is spiritual help within us in the worst of times. It has enabled me to trust other experiences in which spiritual comfort has been more direct.

I awoke alone one morning with a sensation of having been caressed on my cheek. In a dream before awaking, my head was cradled in the lap of a loving presence who was gently stroking my head. His touch on my cheek was felt enough to awaken me—and I believe—was real.

I have never felt alone since having these experiences. Another exercise that has been important to me is one for centering, in which I quietly repeat to myself during meditation, "I am here." After feeling centered within, I announce outside myself—to the room, house, town, country, each continent, the planet and the universe—"I am here," pausing after each place until I am truly there in my imagination. This is a great exercise for the times when I feel fragmented and lost because of the rush of events.

The healing water exercise helps to make concrete the idea that there is a generous, renewable quiet source that feeds our spiritual needs. Whenever I look into that spring in my mind's eye, I feel calm and confident.

Herb has always found his strength and his solace in words. As a writer, especially as a speechwriter, he has learned that words have the power to stir hearts, to change minds, to generate action. This is why, in Chapter six, "Sources of Consolation and Inspiration," he has defined his sources, what works for him, almost entirely in the context of words: poetry, lyrics, aphorisms, essays. Although he has a deep appreciation of the arts, painting, music, dance, and sculpture, the images of ritual have not, for him, had the capacity of words to give him courage and to excite his imagination.

Yet, how can words be divorced from the images they arouse or suggest? How can he recite to himself, for comfort, the Twenty-third Psalm without creating the image of the young shepherd being led beside the still waters, lying down in green pastures, holding God's hand as he walks through the valley of the shadow of death? How can he read Tennyson's *Ulysses* without visualizing that rough, island kingdom of Ithaca, the ancient warrior-king, the crew of hard-bitten old mariners, the ship that would carry them beyond the known margins of the world on their final journey in defiance of fate?

In my work with clients whose lives are threatened by illness, I have approached consolation, inspiration, and healing through images as well as words. In doing so, I believe that, like an increasing number of health professionals, I am utilizing two of the world's oldest and most effective resources for healing: the ancient, nonverbal, free-flowing or *guided imagery* through which an experienced leader (or oneself when practiced) directs the imagination away from self-consciousness to deeper realms of the self; and *visualization*, the self-induced process of using the mind's eye to direct healing energy inward to the source of physical, emotional, or spiritual pain.

For most of the world, and for most of human history, the use of imagination in healing has been a keystone of both Eastern and Western medicine. The great physicians of the past have used imagery in their approach to healing. And even in the practice of modern or scientific medicine, imagery is an internal part of every form of diagnosis and treatment whether the practitioner is aware of it or not.

Within the past two decades, especially, the imagination has regained its primacy in approaches to healing. Guided imagery and visualization, hypnosis, biofeedback, and many other methods have been shown to impact strongly on our autonomic system, to influence our autoimmune processes, and to give us a measure of control over many of our physiological systems such as temperature, heart rate, blood pressure, and more.

According to new research and practice, a variety of techniques—specific images, positive feelings, suggestion, meditation, and relaxation—have demonstrated the potential of increasing the ability of the immune system to counter disease. Properly used, these techniques have the power to alleviate stress and pain and to create a method by which an individual can create a realm of imagination in which there is comfort, safety, inspiration, and alleviation. Imagery, when it is learned and practiced, can generate a whole new world of experience that is freshly and individually created rather than simply a rote response to various textbook diagnoses.

Words play a secondary role in the use of visualization and imaging. By losing oneself in the process, by allowing the imagination to be a guide beyond logic or rationality, beyond words, an altered state of consciousness can be produced in which healing, at last, can take place.

Just as Herb has described some of the words from which he has derived great comfort, pleasure, and inspiration, I am going to describe some exercises and techniques in guided imagery and visualization which I have used both for myself and with clients to create a release from tension, pain, and stress. Over the years, these simple journeys of the imagination have worked for me and my clients, and they are working now for many individuals alone and in groups. I offer them to you especially if you, like Herb, are deeply involved in the preparation for dying. As the substance of your body weakens, your imaging mind can exert its full power and carry you, in tranquility and acceptance, up to and through the gate of death.

The techniques and practices of visualization and guided imagery are not far removed from experiences in daily life that we all share. Sitting in a movie theater, watching television, reading a book, running, playing a sport intensely—in all of these activities we have experienced our ability to suspend consciousness of self, and to remove ourselves completely from the present. As we are totally absorbed in the world of intense concentration, we are carried off in our imagination, through loss of self, to other realms. And when we practice such intentional techniques as yoga or transcendental meditation, we engage in a purposive loss of self-consciousness so that we can experience the healing power of relaxation, imagination, insight, and control of pain or fear.

A few years ago, I was leading two groups in the practice of guided imagery. One was a group of patients living with cancer; the other group was intended for patients with chronic disease, not necessarily life-threatening illness. I was surprised that those persons most threatened by disease showed very little interest in the cancer support group and so, as an experiment, I decided to combine the two groups. The results were immediate. More and more individuals began to attend our meetings and to stay with us. We found that what was most important for all of us, including myself, was to reach beyond the barriers of disease and physical problems to create, in all who participated, a deep, personal sense of well-being and healing, whether our dis-ease was of the body, the mind, the spirit, or in relationships.

What was most interesting to me was that people with a wide variety of impairments were able to benefit in one group, using the same techniques. I discovered that the possibilities for healing through imagery are so open, so amenable to learning and practice, that anyone, whether living with life-threatening illness or not, can learn them and benefit from them. In our groups we demonstrated improvement in outlook, and relief from symptoms of anxiety, lethargy, despair, and hopelessness.

I remember with great fondness a man in his late forties who had been confined to a wheelchair for more than twenty years, having been diagnosed with multiple sclerosis a short time after marrying his childhood sweetheart. The disease had progressed very rapidly. He told me that one of the experiences he missed most by being wheelchair-bound all those years was being able to go dancing with his wife.

We began, then, to use guided imagery in which they danced. These images became quite elaborate in detail. He found great pleasure, whenever he felt like it, in taking these journeys into his imagination. They gave him such joy and happiness. In his mind's eye he could generate for himself, through his active imagination, this experience so long denied him.

I began to call these experiences "vacations in the mind," and I've found that there is no limit to the places we can go: beautiful places we have visited before and to which we want to return; places we've never been but have yearned to see, even imaginary realms we can create in our minds. The possibilities of being released, unbound from the present, are completely open and available. It is such an incredible resource for people who have physical limitations and boundaries—which, in a sense, means all of us.

A few years ago, I had a client with metastasized breast cancer who had a very limited prognosis. A young mother, she was frightened by the prospect of death and how it would rob her and her family. Our work centered on her living. I told her that the matter of dying is something with which each of us must grapple sooner or later. I preferred to deal with dying as part of the natural course of living, of concern to us all, not just to those who have greater awareness of their impending death.

That is why I've found teaching about dying and death to be so gratifying. Many people experience a remarkable liberation from their fear and an enhancement of living with the confrontation and exploration of such a terrifying sub-ject. The young mother came to trust that I was not going to force her to consider her death, something she was not ready to do. We used visualization to help her regain a sense of positive body image. When one's body seems to betray one with the ravages of disease and treatment, it is important to find some comfortable regard and appreciation for it as the only means by which we continue physical existence. I refer to this as "making friends" with one's body.

My client made such gains with this technique that she was able to go shopping for some beautiful, diaphanous nightgowns and resume sexual intimacy with her husband. The use of imagery was also having an effect on her fear of death. As time went on we were able to talk about her death as naturally and freely as we were able to talk about mine. She became acquainted with, familiar with, and eventually trusting of the spiritual core she discovered on her journeys inward. As she worked to repair some significant relation-ships that needed healing, she found a place of love in living that transcended her fear of dying and of death.

Once I visited her in the intensive-care unit. There, the use of imagery helped her again. Her lungs were filling with fluid, and she was very frightened when she had trouble breathing. Of course, her anxiety only exacerbated this condition. As we practiced relaxation and she took time out in her imagery to relive one of her favorite days, she was able to breathe more comfortably and to trust her ability to control her symptoms. Finding a refuge within herself was a surprise to her, and one that allowed her to live without fear in a spiritual dimension she had not experienced before. Soon she came to understand that death would not be the end of her, and this gave her a rich sense of a future that she had not been able to come to through belief in dogma and in faith alone. Through the use of imagery with guidance from someone experienced using it, we can explore incredible depths within and learn to trust the beautiful way in which we are made. We discover that we have resources to bring us to that holy place that is in us, all of us, where on some level of consciousness, our spiritual guidance resides. Eastern forms of meditation teach us that it is safe to let go of self-consciousness, to let go of fear and attachment by having a mini-death that we can induce and trust as a model for eventual bodily death and the continuity of the spirit.

Through visualization and guided imagery we are granted the experience of going to the core of our being, to help us understand more clearly how we are designed, to give us confidence in the ability of our minds to carry us to realms where there is no pain and no fear. Over the years I have learned to respect these techniques and practices, because over and over again I have seen them work.

The visualization can be led by a therapist or guide in person, on a tape, or by oneself using imagination, and after some practice. It is important to know that these exercises can be easily learned and modified to suit one's need or taste.

They can be made very individual. I have practiced these exercises in a number of different settings with many different people leading them. Each of us has our own style. It is fun to create your own adaptations. With practice, anyone can become skilled.

Today, a warm, miraculously sunny day in February, as we were working on this chapter, I led Herb through a complete exercise in guided imagery. After leading him on the path to total relaxation, I brought him through a meadow in his mind, to his inner spirit guide, whom he was to meet in the surrounding forest. I told him to sit on a log awaiting the arrival of his guide, and then to ask him a question whose answer was important to him.

The peace and beauty Herb was able to achieve through this twenty-minute exercise had a profound effect on him, and he knows that he can meet his guide and ask him a question whenever he needs to do so. He has come such a long way since he scoffed at the healing power of imagery and from his disappointment that his first attempts apparently produced no change in the spread of the cancer in his bones. To his regret, he sees now that his skepticism may have cost him a year of inner control through imagery.

For all his skepticism, though, Herb was willing to try anything that would lower the level of anxiety and panic he suffered whenever he had to go to a hospital. Ever since his parents had told him, at the age of three, that he was going to visit his "Uncle Dave" when, in reality, he was going to have his tonsils taken out, Herb has been terrified of hospitals. Today, more than sixty-five years later, he can still smell the sickly, sweet ether, see the nuns in their frightening habits, and, to this terror, repeat his ether dream of two leering goblins on a whirligig, going round and round, grinning evilly at him.

In June 1989, when Herb went to Johns Hopkins Hospital for his initial prostate surgery, his confidence in his physician, Pat Walsh, had a lot to do with his overcoming these long-held, deep-seated fears.

How can I begin to describe how it felt to be taken into Dr. Walsh's skilled and gentle caring after Herb's discouraging diagnosis and inept treatment up to that point. This physician, in the finest sense of the word, cared for Herb and about both of us, and never let us give up hope even when it became evident that through the physician's art alone the disease could not for long be checked. He recognized that healing is a process both of science and of faith, and he was the only doctor we ever met who said he would pray for us.

On the morning of his radical prostatectomy, Herb had to have a diagnostic test in the daunting MRI (Magnetic Resonance Imaging) machine. This is a long, narrow tube into which the patient is placed, to the accompaniment of flashing lights, vibrations, and darkness. Fellow patients told Herb how frightful the experience was for them. One had actually suffered a claustrophobic panic attack of such intensity that the test had to be abandoned.

I told Herb that this would not happen to him if, when placed in the machine, he took himself out of the present through imagery. I suggested that he recite his favorite poetry, as he recalls every poem he's memorized since childhood, or to place himself in a past favorite day or location he would like to explore again.

When he was back in his room, calm and smiling, I knew he had been successful. "What did you do?" I asked.

"Well," he answered, "I wanted to get as far as possible from that dark tube, and so, once inside, I began to tell myself and project myself into old, familiar nursery tales. *The Three Bears* was followed by *Little Red Riding Hood,* and by the time the hunters killed the wolf, the procedure was over, and I had felt no fear."

This experience gave him a tremendous psychological boost. So much so that he needed no sedation before being taken to the operating room. The only precondition he had set was that he would not have the anesthesia administered by face mask. As they wheeled him into the brightly illuminated surgical theater, he began to sing. Dr. Walsh told me later that, for a moment, he thought Herb was becoming hysterical. But Herb had gathered so much courage from the earlier imagery experience that he was in a calm, serene world of his own making. He sang "When Irish Eyes Are Smiling" to Dr. Walsh, ending with ". . . sure they steal your prostate away."

When I was allowed to see him briefly in the recovery room just after I was told with kindness but with certainty that Herb's cancer had spread beyond the prostate and so was indeed metastatic, he greeted me in the hushed silence with a booming, cheery, "I'm over here, dear!" Needless to say, there was no trace of panic in him. Just the opposite. His recovery was quick, the healing of the surgical wounds and the restoration of bodily functions almost miraculously without pain or discomfort.

Between June 1989 and January 1990, when he had to undergo castration, he continued to use visualization techniques, scouring rib and pelvic bones where cancer sites were found. According to Herb, the cancer cells gleamed like

President Bush's "thousand points of light." "I projected my mind into these crowded areas of my skeleton and simply told those cells to vanish, NOW!" They vanished for a time, and he felt he had triumphed over them. And, finally, as he came back to consciousness after the orchiectomy, Herb serenaded Dr. Walsh with a chorus of "After the Balls Were Over," his earthy version of an old popular song written by his great-uncle Charles K. Harris.

Chapter Five

DREAMS
AND
VISIONS

A categorical question is being put to [a dying man,] and he is under an obligation to answer it. To this end he ought to have a myth about death, for reason shows him nothing but the dark pit into which he is descending. Myth, however, can conjure up other images for him, helpful and enriching pictures of life in the land of the dead. If he believes in them, or greets them with some measure of credence, he is being just as right or just as wrong as someone who does not believe in them. But while the man who despairs marches toward nothingness, the one who has placed his faith in the archetype follows the tracks of uncertainty, but the one lives against his instincts, the other with them. *

*Carl Jung, *Memories, Dreams, Reflections.*

As the life of the physical world becomes sparser and more difficult for me because of my disease, the world of dreams, visions, and mystical experiences opens out into landscapes I have never perceived before, landscapes of richness and wonder that seem to presage the wonder to be.

In various conversations in this book, I have referred to some of these dreams and visions: the dream of a God who created the universe because He dreamed of a garden; the Tibetan monks who gave me my mantra, "Nothing dies"; the dreams of radiance, of healing, of light.

Increasingly, however, my dreams have become what seems to me to be an intervention—from what source I do not know—by other-worldly spirits who, now that death is much nearer at hand, are sending me, perhaps from my own unconscious, specific images of protection and love.

Dominating my dream world for the past month or so has been the repeated appearance of a mysterious robed figure whose gentle touch and loving embrace have not only been experienced in dream images, but have actually been felt tactilely. In this way, in body as well as in mind, or from whatever realm dreams flow, I have been given physical evidence that the dream is real.

The first time I saw and felt the presence of this mysterious stranger was between Thanksgiving and Christmas. I was half asleep, almost unconscious, in the large chair in the living room where I spend most of my days. As I drifted off, I actually felt that I was being lifted up out of my chair by a lofty, humanesque "creature" dressed in a flowing gray garment with a hood or cowl concealing his face. I knew that he was male, very tall, strong, but gentle. Without effort he lifted me from the chair and gathered me into his arms. All

of this I could feel as well as witness, as I experienced physically the lifting, the embrace, the texture of the coarse,
flowing garment. I knew it was not merely a figment of my
imagination. It was really happening. And though by now I
believe I was fully asleep, I felt the sensation of being returned to my chair from the height of his embrace.

While in that first dream I did not associate the figure
with anything specifically angelic, somehow I knew he was
intimately involved in my life as a guide or angel-like being.
I sensed that he was inexorably bound to my fate here on
earth and on my journey through the portal of death. I
sensed strongly that at this stage of my dying, he had chosen
to make himself manifest to me as a physical presence.

About two or three weeks after this first appearance, I
was once again visited in a dream by the "creature" in the
gray robe. This time, however, he did not lift me from the
chair, but, instead, pushed back the hood as he bent over
me, revealing a strong, lined, compassionate face, dark hair,
and piercing blue eyes. He looked at me for a moment and
then vanished.

A week or so later, he returned in my dream, and once
again I felt his tender ministrations with my body as well as
in a dream image. He was seated in a large chair, like the
Daniel Chester French statue of Abraham Lincoln, and he
held me in his lap, cradling me, holding me tight, until once
again, he stood up, then set me down in what was my own
chair. But, as he set me down, I looked around and saw
folded against his back, emerging from his body, two strong,
white feathered wings. So clear was this vision that I could
see in minute detail the powerful muscles at the base of the
wings and the shape and symmetry of every feather as they

moved slightly in the ambient air of the room. And I remember thinking, even as I saw and felt his presence, that the appearance of the wings was a sign to me that he was indeed a guardian angel who will protect me from harm in my dying. And I knew that the wings were probably made visible so that I would be reassured of his benevolence through the use of a conventional image that would not cause me even more anxiety. Two nights ago (I am writing on January 27, 1992), I had the most powerful and emotionally stirring dream of the person I now recognize as a guardian angel.

I was climbing the last few feet of the steep path that ascends the mountain Kay and I have climbed so often at Rancho La Puerto in Tecate, Mexico. It was a beautiful morning with the sun rising, and every detail of the rocks, the feature for which this place is most famous, was thrown into relief. At the end of the vertical trail is a horizontal, rock-strewn path leading back down the other side of the mountain to the fields and streams below. Not being certain of my destination, I sat down on a flat rock and drank in the light and the warmth and the mystery of those ancient carved boulders. As I sat there, I realized how tired I really was, so I rested my head on my hands and waited for the fatigue to pass.

Suddenly, I felt that I was not alone and saw coming down the path toward me the robed but once again wingless figure of my "guardian angel." At first, I thought that the figure emerging from the light behind him was a representation of Christ. But as he came closer I knew, even with the bright sun at his back, that it was, indeed, my guide and guardian.

He approached me silently, and drawing a bottle and a spoon from his robe, he filled the spoon and held it out toward me. "Take this," he said. "It will ease your pain." He approached my mouth with the spoon, and I awoke with my mouth open to receive it, and my tongue moving to accept it, just like a nestling receiving food from its mother.

I felt, as I awoke, a great sense of peace and wonder, but also tremendous sadness. And I could not tell Kay about the dream without tears. This was the second time I had dreamed of receiving some kind of nourishment from a stranger, though I don't remember the details of the first, save the robed arm reaching out toward me.

Along more conventional lines, if dreams can ever be conventional, I dreamed recently that I was asleep on my bed when suddenly, four traditional angels, white robes, wings and all, appeared at the bed's four corners. Each lifted a corner of the sheet and held me high, beating their wings until they put me softly back on the bed. I knew it was only a dream, but it filled me with a great sense of peace and lightness.

Without being overly analytical about these dreams, it seems obvious to me that as death approaches, something changes dramatically in the relationship between our conscious and unconscious selves and between us, who are death-bound, and the universe itself. This is why the richness of Carl Jung's psychology is so much more satisfying to me than what I take to be, though I am no scholar in it, Freud's more limited mapping of the self and its components. For example, I could not possibly explain to myself various dreams of animals I have had recently if I knew nothing of

Jung's concept of the "shadow," the baser self which, on re-flection, these animals so obviously represent.

A few weeks ago, I dreamed I was here at home, that safe, familiar, peaceful place, when suddenly there was a ter-rible commotion, and the peace was shattered by the inva-sion of a large, grunting, pink pig. I could see every detail of the pig's huge, obscenely gross body and hear its grunts as it rushed through the house, overturning furniture, pushing everything and everyone before it. The pig itself, while beau-tiful in a way in its sleek pinkness, was an object more of fear than of fascination.

When I awoke, filled with the sights and sounds of the pig's invasion, I realized that the pig represented two aspects of myself at this time. It was the cancer thrusting through the marrow of my bones, squeezing before it the source of life-creating red blood cells and pushing everything else out of its way. But the pig was also a representation of my intru-sion, as a dying man, into this beautiful place, the home into which I have already, consistently brought such chaos over these past twelve years. So, in my own interpretation of Jung, the animals of my dreams represent the baser, selfish, dark side of my nature as well as the grossness of what I am now being asked, by external nature, to suffer until I reach some higher plane of living. And it is this promise of release from the shadow that I feel certain is what the an-gelic visitations are all about.

The pig was not the last of my animal visitations. Last night, as I lay in bed, I was certain that I heard the pawing and snuffling of a large brown bear that was trying to gain access to my sanctuary. As the bear approached the door, suddenly I heard the growling of our calico cat. I have a radio on a night table next to my bed, and I could hear the cat's warning growls above the sound of the radio. Even though I realized, when I awoke, that I had been dreaming, the sound of the cat and the reality of its protective presence were so vivid that I had to turn on the light to see for myself whether or not the cat was really there.

When I told Kay about the dream, she said, "You know how I am always talking to our animals. Well, yesterday afternoon, I told Betty Friedan [our cat's name] to stay very near you and to protect you. I guess we're now involving our pets in our circle of extrasensory perception."

Since I am dreaming so vividly almost every night, this chapter could go on and on until the final dream takes me from my bed and from this world. And so the dream I am about to recount will be the last I will record. The point I would make is that throughout the dying process, dreams, at least in my case, have become more realistic, more memorable, linked to very spiritual themes, reflecting my need for love, protection, safety, and assurance of a realm beyond the door. None, until last night, has had conventional religious imagery, and I can trace the source of that in my reading of the Bible yesterday (not a usual occurrence, I might add).

The day had been very traumatic, even explosive. I had fallen and hurt my ribs and the pain medication had "put me out" at about six o'clock in the evening. I fell asleep immediately, and I dreamed I was on the rocky, forbidding plain where Jesus was crucified. I was seated at the foot of the cross. Looking up, I could see him writhing in pain and hear his groans. Drops of his blood were falling on me. Then suddenly, I was in my own bed. I heard a voice that said, "It won't be long."

Something told me to look at my hands. The angry red blotches of broken capillaries were fading from my wrists. I had associated them with stigmata. I awoke in a cold sweat with the fear that I was going to be "taken" that very night.

Somehow, I went back to sleep again and dreamed that the telephone was ringing. In my dream I got out of bed to answer it. No one was on the line. I kept saying, "Hello. Hello," until finally the silence was broken, a soft whispered voice said, "Not yet," and the caller hung up.

As I said at the outset, I have never had a rich, stirring dream life. Our game of "Herr Dr. Freud and Herr Dr. Jung" is fueled by Kay's dreams, not mine, and I don't know enough about dying people to generalize on the recent experiences I have had.

But I can say that dreams now come more frequently and are remembered the next day and for days to come. The dreams are more directly linked to my condition and my fate. Above all, they are not nightmares of death, but visions of comfort and safety. And I am thrilled, whether or not it was my own wishful thinking that transmitted the whispered message, that the last words I heard on the dream telephone were, "Not yet."

Chapter Six

SOURCES OF CONSOLATION AND INSPIRATION

I T IS ALMOST THREE YEARS since my sentence of death was pronounced by the much-too-busy-for-feeling urologist. It is almost one year since Kay and I began this adventure in sharing our insights and experiences with the unfolding drama of dying, facing death, and understanding the spiritual journey on which we are embarked. Sometimes, it has seemed we are traveling together, as Kay has guided me from fear and doubt to a place of safety and resolution—and sometimes it seems we are moving almost in opposite directions, as my journey of the spirit, coupled with my growing physical dependence, has interrupted and contradicted her hopes, expectations, and the quality of her life.

In all this time of learning, growing, and sharing, my greatest consolation and inspiration have come from Kay, who has answered my questions, stilled my doubts, and calmed my fears. How she attained such wisdom and resolved her own doubts and fears is still not clear to me. But

what she has said, and the loving care and courageous outlook she has demonstrated throughout these past three years,
ring absolutely true. I find in her no dogma, no phony religi-
osity or quick-fix, pop psychologizing. Her power comes, as
does her healing, from her passionate belief in the continuity
of the spirit, in a larger universal purpose and being which
we all share, and in the ultimate good. In her convictions,
there is no base metal. They are pure gold. One does not
have to agree with her metaphysics to feel the healing power
of her beliefs. I wish her gentle voice could be heard beyond
the confines of my room, my mind, my journey. I wish it
could be heard by you.

But along the way, there have been other voices, other
sources of consolation and inspiration—snippets of poetry,
the words of philosophers and mystics, the ruminations of
scientists and scholars who have created a constant, re-
freshing source of certainty, beauty, and belief. Their words
offer testimony that validates and enriches what Kay has
given to me, even as they have opened up new and different
vistas of the same unifying truth.

As my last contribution to the record of this adventure,
which is now drawing to its inevitable close, I offer some of
these voices which, every day, have buttressed my courage,
livened my imagination, and joined with Kay and me in an
uplifting chorus of faith and hope.

To an extent, of course, I am culture-bound. My long
experience in teaching and learning has been centered for
the most part on the Judaeo-Christian tradition and on An-
glo-European culture. During these past months and years,
however, I have read and heard much that has been inspired
by other traditions and other cultures: Joseph Campbell; the

Tibetan Book of the Dead; Lao-tse; the *Bhagavad-Gita,* and other monuments of lives and cultures distant in both time and place. Most of these non-Western sources Kay has brought to me from her own study, which has ranged far beyond my own.

Let me not pretend that I have understood or even been moved by everything I have heard and seen. Some of these works have been simply too remote from my own experience to be fully appreciated or even comprehended. But even from these, I have drawn much that rings true, that inspires and encourages, like the vision of the Tibetan monks, who, in my waking dream, amid the sounding of gongs and the whirring of prayer wheels, gave me the mantra I was seeking, "Nothing dies."

And I can't pretend that every day, because of the strength I have drawn from Kay and other sources cited, has been free of anxiety and doubt. This would testify to an unnatural absence of feeling. God knows, we have both lived through roller-coasters of emotion these last months, especially since the Suramin failed.

Yesterday, I returned home from two weeks in the hospital to whose emergency room I was brought early on New Year's Day 1992. I awakened at three o'clock in the morning suffering from an outbreak of physical pain whose like I had not experienced since this journey began. It was a low blow to hope and to optimism. But it is satisfying, in the depths, to be able to repeat words like, "This, too, shall pass," and "Take this cup from me," that resonate back through time to the greater suffering of greater beings who brought consolation and inspiration to the whole world.

Though these days are not, I believe, anything more

than the long overture to the final act, I cannot help but recognize that events are speeding us toward the conclusion and that sooner, rather than later, to quote another fragment of folk wisdom, "The fat lady will sing," and the curtain will come down.

I know I will have enough strength as well as the absence of suffering to complete this book, even as, in the words of the seventeenth-century poet Andrew Marvell, "At my back I always hear/Time's winged chariot drawing near." And with a rueful smile I can recognize with him that though "the grave's a fine and private place/None I think do there embrace"—words that probably enticed many a "coy mistress" to his bed.

Although my own brain is cluttered with a lifetime of words, stanzas, whole poems, and the choruses of popular songs, I do not intend this chapter to be anything more than a patchwork of scattered sources from which I have drawn comfort and security as well as great pleasure.

Since the beginning of my journey toward death, I have kept a notebook of fragments and entire works that have become sources of consolation and inspiration. One rule is that these *not* be limited to what are usually considered "great thoughts from great thinkers." Whatever stirs, whatever moves, whether to laughter or to tears, has been included and as much memorized as possible, because one never knows when he will have the need for expressions ranging from "As long as I can be with you, it's a lovely day" (which, as sung by Fred Astaire, will be the recessional at my funeral), to "I am the master of my fate, I am the captain of my soul," from William Ernest Henley's "Invictus." Heywood Broun has called "Invictus" the third-most-annoying poem in his experience, the other two being Joyce Kilmer's "Trees" and Rudyard Kipling's "If." So what. If they help you, make the lines yours.

As I've said many times, the words that bring me the most comfort, day by day, are those simple, pastoral lines of the Twenty-third Psalm which seem to link my own life, not with a specific, Old Testament deity, but with the purpose and meaning of the universe. I'm not a Biblical scholar or even "religious" in a formal sense, but these words sung by that young shepherd boy thousands of years ago speak directly to my soul in its time of darkest need.

> Yea, though I walk through the valley of the
> shadow of death, I will fear no evil, for Thou art
> with me;
> Thy rod and Thy staff, they comfort me.
> Thou preparest a table before me in the presence
> of mine enemies;
> Thou annointest my head with oil; my cup
> runneth over.
> Surely goodness and mercy shall follow me all the
> days of my life;
> And I will dwell in the house of the Lord forever.

These lines seem to connect me to every person, every creature, every plant and star. For when one is on one's own walk through the "valley of the shadow of death" and fears no evil and feels no fear, can one doubt that the "Lord," whoever or whatever that is, has taken his hand and is guiding him to the revelation of the ultimate mystery?

Of course, there are hundreds of gorgeous poems and

prayers in the Old and New Testaments that we can all call upon in time of need. The Psalms, especially, are so direct, so pure in their reverence for the God "that has made us and not we ourselves," that I frequently dip into the Bible and draw from it new respect for these ancient poets and prophets. But I cannot take scriptures as the revealed word of God, and I cannot accept the straitjacket of sectarian dogma that both Judaism and Christianity, to my mind, have become. So I draw most of my consolation and inspiration from poets and philosophers who do not have a creed to sell—whose words are truly intuitive, making no demands that we subscribe to their every syllable as representing some higher truth. That is why my own notebook is far more secular than sectarian. It is from the poets I draw most nurture.

So much of so-called "modern" poetry is so privately symbolic, so intellectual, so closed to simple, direct expression of emotion that few modern poets are sources of real comfort when grief and doubt close in. And so, in terms of time, I am pretty much stuck in the years up to the midpoint of this century; and in style, I find conventional verse most directly available and affecting. Let's face it: I am most moved by those who have intentionally set out to move me with the beauty of their words and the simple, direct expressions of their own emotions.

For example, I carry both in my head and in my notebook many lines and verses of Alfred, Lord Tennyson, whose thought, though considered by many modernists to be hopelessly outdated, moves me almost as much as the beauty of his verse. When I think of my own immediate death, I derive great peace and stillness from a poem like "Crossing the Bar," which on its own terms speaks to me as simply and persuasively as the song of the young shepherd boy. The four short verses of "Crossing the Bar" often float through my consciousness in fragments or in their entirety. The poem never fails to stir powerful emotions of reverence, longing, peace:

> Sunset and evening star,
> And one clear call for me!
> And may there be no moaning of the bar,
> When I put out to sea,
>
> But such a tide as moving seems asleep,
> Too full for sound and foam,
> When that which drew from out the boundless deep
> Turns again home.
>
> Twilight and evening bell,
> And after that the dark!
> And may there be no sadness of farewell,
> When I embark;
>
> For tho' from out our bourne of Time and Place
> The flood may bear me far,
> I hope to see my Pilot face to face
> When I have crost the bar.

This longing to see God's face, and the poetic if not the theological certainty that one will, after death, also informs these lovely lines of Emily Dickinson:

> I never saw a moor
> I never saw the sea.

Yet know I how the heather looks
and what a wave must be.

I have never spoke to God
Nor visited in heaven
Yet certain am I of the spot
As if the chart were given.

Of all poets, certainly within a century or so, Emily
Dickinson's expression of faith in things unseen is most simple and direct. Her clear-eyed honesty reminds me of Kay.
From the isolation of her room, Dickinson could see
truth—human and divine, with the naked eye. And she
knew death intimately long before she found it herself:

The world feels dusty
When we stop to die;
We want the dew then,
Honors taste dry.

Flags vex a dying face,
But the least fan
Stirred by a friend's hand
Cools like rain.

Mine be thy ministry
When the thirst comes,
Dews of thyself to fetch
And holy balms.

The above lines, which reveal to us the superiority of
the grace of caring to the glory of accomplishment, so often

remind me of the lines in Thomas Gray's "Elegy in a Country Churchyard":

> The boast of heraldry, the pomp of pow'r,
> And all that beauty, all that wealth e'er gave,
> Awaits alike the inevitable hour:
> The paths of glory lead but to the grave.

It is this truth, answered too late (if only I had listened to my poets), which has enabled me so effortlessly to let go of the frenetic quest for earthly accomplishments and to recognize that the paths of meditation, of insight, of failure even, lead us ultimately to the place where our models and our bank accounts mean nothing.

And this, in turn, often leads me to remember and recite the words of the contemporary English poet Philip Larkin. In "An Arundel Tomb," he tells of seeing, in the church, the tomb of the countess and the earl who had once ruled that place. The stone of the tomb has eroded. There are only faint traces of the splendor of their clothing: his armor, her robes, their wealth of possessions as they lie together over the centuries, side by side in the tomb. "Side by side, their faces blurred, the Earl and Countess lie in stone," he begins. And he concludes with:

> Time has transfigured them into Untruth
> The stone fidelity
> They hardly meant has come to be
> The final blazon, and to prove
> Our almost instinct almost true:
> What will survive of us is love.

W. H. Auden responds to these humble "almosts" with the certitude that "We must love one another or die." By this, of course, the poet means a death of the spirit in this world. For we all must come to the door and pass beyond, and what survives of us—as far as we can know—is the power of our love, which transcends all loss and calms all grief. It is written in the *Bhagavad-Gita,* that supreme holy story from ancient India:

> For certain is death for the born
> And certain is birth for the dead.
> Therefore over the inevitable
> Thou shouldst not grieve.

The above, in turn, reminds me of another of my favorite Tennysonia—"Ulysses." In this great narrative, Tennyson tells of the hero of the Trojan wars, Ulysses, who, returning from his great adventures, has grown weary of sitting idly on the throne of a tiny island kingdom waiting to die. So he rallies his old shipmates and urges them to come with him on one last, bold foray—beyond the known world, right up to the gates of death. Calling them to action, he says:

> 'Tis not too late to seek a newer world . . .
> It may be that the gulfs will wash us down;
> It may be we shall touch the Happy Isles,
> And see the great Achilles, whom we knew.
> Tho' much is taken, much abides; and tho'
> We are not now that strength which in the old
> days

Moved earth and heaven, that which we are, we
are,—
One equal temper of heroic hearts,
Made weak by time and fate, but strong in will
To strive, to seek, to find, and not to yield.

How many times have I quoted those lines to force myself to press on jubilantly, when the courage to go on was
failing. And the sentiment, this need not to give in, not to
submit to the inevitable, is echoed in Robert Frost's familiar,
but little understood, lines from "Stopping by Woods on a
Snowy Evening":

The woods are lovely, dark and deep.
But I have promises to keep,
And miles to go before I sleep,
And miles to go before I sleep.

I say "little understood," because I think this poem is
more than a bucolic interlude. It is about death, about the
sweet tension between the lovely, long slumber of death and
the need to fulfill promises made in this realm, as we discussed in our final conversation, "Coming Home."

Since this is not a scholarly exercise or a test of either
taste or memory, I am not ashamed to go to a *Bartlett's* or
other books of familiar quotations and look up the subjects
(love, death, courage, hope, etc.) that will best lift my spirits. There I can find not only great lines and familiar aphorisms, but often whole poems to copy in my notebook. Nor
do all these sources need some official stamp of "greatness."

For example: Often, among all these magnificent affirmations of abiding love as the ultimate purpose of life and of eternity, Kay and I have found ourselves singing songs like that resounding shower-bath ballad, Victor Herbert's "Ah, Sweet Mystery of Life":

> For 'tis love and love alone the world is seeking,
> For 'tis love and love alone that can repay—
> 'Tis the answer, 'tis the end and all of living,
> For it is love alone that rules for aye.

And then I've often repeated from Paul's letter to the Corinthians, "And now abideth faith, hope, and love, but the greatest of these is love,"—which Elizabeth Barrett Browning amplifies with her all-too-familiar, but still powerful sonnet that begins, "How do I love thee? Let me count the ways." It ends:

> . . . I love thee with the breath,
> Smiles, tears, of all my life!—and, if God choose,
> I shall but love thee better after death.

To which Robert Browning answered with his own magnificent affirmation of eternal life and love, "Prospice," written after her death. And so the source is enriched and enlarged again.

For how can one be defeated (Corinthians, "O death, where is thy sting? O grave, where is thy victory?") or cower before death's grim visage (John Donne's "Death, be not proud . . ."), with such glowing touchstones to throw as a challenge to invader death? And if this all begins to sound too sentimental, too emotional in the face of scientific proof, I recall the words of our greatest scientist, Albert Einstein, who said—and this I have to read from my notebook:

> A person who is religiously enlightened appears to me to be one who has to the best of his ability, liberated himself from the fetters of his selfish desires and is preoccupied with thoughts and feelings and aspirations to which he clings because of their super-personal value.

When people chide Kay and me for what they take to be an unsupported, irrational view of life, death, and the universe, we can say with Einstein, "Science without religion is lame. Religion without science is blind." One cannot view life and death and their meaning through only one lens. Religious dogma is as blind as scientific dogma is lame. And this thought takes me to one of my favorite poems by Walt Whitman—its first line is its title:

> When I heard the learn'd astronomer,
> When the proofs, the figures were raised in columns before me,
> When I was shown the charts and diagrams, to add, divide, and measure them,
> When I sitting heard the astronomer where he lectured with much applause in the lecture-room,
> How soon unaccountable I became tired and sick,
> Till rising and gliding out I wander'd off by myself
> In the mystical moist night-air, and from time to time

Look'd up in perfect silence at the stars.

How often, at Cape Cod, have we stood in the absolute darkness and stillness and marveled at the incredible beauty of the stars? How did this mystery come to be? Then I read "The Creation," by James Weldon Johnson, who, long before my dream of God's longing for a garden, placed God in the emptiness of His own dream, a dream born of loneliness:

> And God stepped out in space,
> And He looked around and said,
> "I'm lonely—
> I'll make me a world."

And so He created the light out of darkness, and all the world to be warmed by the light and the creatures of earth and water and sky, and finally:

> Then God walked around
> And God looked around
> On all that He had made.
> He looked at his sun,
> And He looked at His moon,
> And He looked at the little stars;
> He looked on His world
> With all its living things,
> And God said, "I'm lonely still."

> Then God sat down
> On the side of a hill where He could think;
> By a deep, wide river He sat down;
> With his head in his hands,

God thought and thought,
Till He thought, "I'll make me a man!"

It is then that I hear the unmistakable voice of Louis Armstrong singing in my inner ear: ". . . what a wonderful world." Or hear the duet of Billy Eckstine and Woody Herman: "Life is just a bowl of cherries. Don't take it serious, it's too mysterious . . ."

Every day and in the lonely dark, I take consolation and inspiration from those who have come before us and guide us still. And I try not to be sad or downcast, for as White Eagle says in *The Still Voice*, "It is so important to be balanced in your spiritual life. You may devote your life to spiritual service, but this doesn't mean a life of gloom. No, you radiate joy and light." That is what, during most of this journey, I have tried to do.

And so it comes full circle. "Surely goodness and mercy shall follow me all the days of my life; and I will dwell in the house of the Lord forever." And having reassured myself of this, I usually repeat, before I sleep, the words of Paul's Epistle to Timothy: "I have fought a good fight. I have finished my course. I have kept the faith."

AFTERWORD

O N APRIL 9, 1992, AT 5:05 P.M., HERB DIED. The inevitable for which he had so courageously prepared occurred as he had wished and hoped, at home, naturally, gently, in a circle of loving family members and friends, his hand in mine.

The previous day, at the hematology unit at St. Francis Hospital, where he went several times a week for monitoring, Heidi and I were told by his dearly loved nurse, Fay Ewen, that it was a matter of days. I told this to Herb, adding that this was not the time to stop being candid with each other about what was happening or to close ourselves to the experience we had faced with such openness so far. He said simply, "I'm ready."

When we got home, he wanted to undress and get in bed. The last couple of weeks had been difficult for him. Increasingly weakened from the disease and not being able to swallow easily, for the first time, he experienced what seemed to be intense grief about his losses.

Energy was something he had always had in abundance. When it began to wane, there was still that enormous mental energy that kept his intellect coursing ahead with interest and curiosity, causing him to say a few weeks before that the smaller his body got, the bigger he felt.

The next day, the day he died, was the first time he did not get up to dress. It was as if he had resigned himself to what was happening and, with the usual full-speed-ahead with which he approached everything else, had simply decided to get on with it.

In the morning some dear friends, the Schwolskys, came to see him. With him, they reviewed the George Bernard Shaw play which Herb had miraculously sat through for three hours a few days earlier at the Hartford Stage Company. Although fatigued, he was able to engage in characteristically amusing and sharp banter with his friends.

About noon, I left him to see a client. He just seemed tired. Nancy sat with him because he had asked not to be left alone. When I came downstairs after the session, he had deteriorated drastically and was barely able to talk.

The vigil began, with his only remaining response being to move when I asked him to help me turn him. After three o'clock he was no longer able to move. He seemed to be in a peaceful, deep sleep. We gathered and sat in silence most of the time after that, until a twitch of his lip signaled the end was at hand.

Then it was over. So quickly, easily, simply, gently. I held his hand and cried quietly for a long time.

It's amazing what we are able to do when we behave in a natural and centered way. An inner voice seemed to direct and guide me through the next few hours with a certainty and calm that enabled me to know and to do just what needed to be done.

Not ready to surrender the sight and presence of his body, I directed that it would remain in the house overnight and that it would be buried the next day. There was no doubt that this was what I wanted to do.

With candles, Native American chanting music in the background, gifts and cards placed about him, we greeted friends and relatives to share this sacred time of passing. Tears and laughter and chatting and the ordinary business of the house went on about him in such a natural way that it did not occur to me until afterward that people coming to the house might be surprised to see his body in full view.

At eleven o'clock, Caroline conducted a ceremony de-rived from a Native American tradition. Western sage and juniper, both cleansing herbs, were burned to prepare Herb's spirit to move on to its new journey. The spirits of the six directions were called on to guide him on his way. We each spoke to his spirit and prayed.

The next morning I awoke before dawn and sat with him until the last candle flickered out and the sun was up.

When the undertaker came for his body later in the morning, he asked if we wanted to leave the room while the body was prepared for removal. Remarkably, the children and I answered in unison, "No." We stood vigil. When it was time for him to leave, each one of us gave him a farewell kiss. We accompanied his body out the door and onto the porch, where we all watched in silence as the hearse drove off down the street.

Leaning against the porch pillar, I wept as I remem-bered the sight of him the first time he appeared at this door, the romantic arrivals during our brief courtship, the evening he arrived for our marriage ceremony, and all the times he left, usually racing at breakneck speed for Mr. Duncan's cab—coat, hat, and bag already airborne for his trip to the airport—and on to Washington in the early morning hours before the rest of the street was awake. I could see him running out the door to ride the new bike I got him on his sixtieth birthday, and the surprise on his face the time the white limousine came to pick him up for a Father's Day picnic at Gillette Castle.

It felt as if my heart were breaking as I watched him leave this street for the last time, this street he loved, that looked so good to him each time he returned to it after every journey, this street that was home to him since 1953.

The day before he died I lay down with him on his bed while he rested. The radio played softly in the background. Trying to place the familiar opera, I asked him what it was. He whispered, "Wagner." I said, "Yes, but which one?" He replied impatiently, "Please, dear. Not now!" It was as if he was annoyed at being interrupted from the important task of dying. It was the first time I ever remembered his not eagerly answering a question. He loved questions. He loved asking them, being asked them. He loved finding answers to questions. This signaled the beginning of his withdrawal from me.

The dialogue that began during our first visit in his living room across the street on June 26, 1980, and that had continued, nonstop, at all hours in all the intervening days and nights, from all locations wherever there were telephones or mail delivery, paused briefly for a time.

On the day of the memorial service, April 15, as I was getting dressed, I experienced a feeling of deep guilt. Had I loved him enough? Had I told him enough? Done enough? The last weeks had been so hard. When I received a letter in the mail the week before saying the IRS was auditing us because of his business expenses, I became enraged at him for his lax record keeping and his ignoring my requests that he do better. Now, on this day, as I reached into my bureau drawer for a hairbrush, a yellow lined, folded piece of paper saying "To Kay" was on top of the assorted stuff that mysteriously finds its way into that place. It was a note I vaguely remembered Herb having given me some weeks earlier.

It was a direct answer to the questions I was now asking. In his beautiful words and style, he not only answered my question, he managed to give me yet another love letter, and a sign that he was with me, encouraging me, forgiving me, thanking me, and loving me.

A few days later at our favorite restaurant in Provincetown, he made his presence known to us again. After the waitress took our drink order, my children and I sat in quietness with our own thoughts. I said, "You know, I miss him. I just miss HIM." The waitress returned and put our drinks down in front of us and said, "The bartender made this cranberry juice by mistake, but he said to give it to you anyway." Cranberry juice was the only drink Herb ever ordered.

Soon our paths will diverge, but not yet.

The first time Herb mentioned that he wanted to write a book was when we were on vacation in Switzerland. Recently, I found the original outline in Herb's writing on a large dinner napkin. It was entitled, *Facing Death*. I was amazed to find that that outline varies little from what now exists.

We were hiking down from Kleine Scheidegg to Wengen on one of the steeper mountain paths through a tall stand of trees when a thunderstorm began. As lightning crackled around us, we prayed not to be hit while we scurried ahead, there being no safe place to stop. After a few minutes we came to a meadow clearing and found shelter in a small barn. Other hikers shared the safety of this dark place with us. When the storm had passed, we walked to a nearby rest station, with the unlikely name of Mary's Café. It was there that we began to talk about writing a book together and there where he scribbled that first outline on a dinner napkin.

It was Herb's idea to write a book about my work and his experience thinking about death. At this point he seemed to have little emotional connection with the idea of his own death, even though it was always with us. As I recited what I thought the contents of such a book should include, I remember having mixed feelings.

I was angry that Herb had metastatic disease that I thought would kill him. That this terrible event was the motivation for our writing a book made talking about my work suddenly annoying. Yet, there he was, with his usual enthusiasm, contemplating a new assignment with the usual eagerness.

Eventually, as time went on, I began to feel excited by his energy and enthusiasm. So many times I watched with amazement as he magically researched and brilliantly wrote on all sorts of subjects about which he knew nothing firsthand. This would be different.

That was the summer of 1990. There were still many months ahead of vigor and seeming health and very little perception on Herb's part that he was ill. When the disease signaled its growing presence in the spring of 1991, he began to write.

For him, it was the book he had always wanted to write but had been unable to do. We often talked about why he had not written in his own name before and found no answers in the deep mystery of his psyche, where it was determined that instead he would write other people's words for them.

It's ironic that he would find his voice in the event of his death. Once found, however, he reveled in it and felt that he did some of his best writing. A well had opened within him, and he continued to write beautiful poetry and prose until a few days before his death.

He said he loved working under a deadline. I asked if he had to take it to this extreme. We worked together easily. There were never any arguments or temper tantrums. He said this was unusual in a husband and wife writing team, and thought we would have a great future together writing, if only he had a future.

Writing this book not only opened Herb's voice for him, it opened up the process of thinking and struggling that resulted in his coming to terms with a much feared death that had been the source of panic attacks about dying throughout his life. He thought seriously, really seriously, for the first time about trusting some of his subjective experiences, found a framework in which to understand them, and discovered a whole new dimension of spirituality that he had longed for but never known before.

As our friend Larry Leamer, who spoke at Herb's memorial service, said,

Herb did not go gently into that good night. Yet he did not rage, rage at the dying of the light. As the light died, he looked at the shadows, at the flickering remnants of the light, and he put down on pages what it was like.

Near the end Herb asked his inner guide one last time, "When?" His guide answered, "Soon." We accepted this gentle answer and cried.

I have used many films and books done by people who have needed to share their experiences with dying and death. Beyond the obvious personal benefits in doing it, we must do it for each other. What happened for Herb can happen for anyone open to learning and growing in this life event we all share called death.

GUIDED IMAGERY EXERCISES

W E START WITH A RELAXATION EXERCISE that helps us to turn inward by directing awareness to each part of the body. Some techniques focus on the breath, some on releasing tension in the muscles. But all have the objective of complete relaxation for the journey to come.

It is necessary, at the outset, to feel comfortable and completely supported. If you are seated, the chair on which you are sitting should be firm; your feet should make good contact with the floor, legs uncrossed. With your back straight, your head is comfortably supported by the spine. You should be aware of your "sitz bones" and be comfortably balanced on them. You may want to practice until you find your correct sitting posture. You want to have the feeling of being held in perfect support and balance. Your arms should be placed comfortably in your lap or at your side.

The subjective impression should be one of attentiveness, anticipation, and restful waiting. For people who must remain in bed or who are reclining, it is important to feel comfortable throughout the whole body. Once the proper position is taken and the relaxation exercise done, the imagery or visualization should range from five to twenty minutes' duration.

To begin an exercise in guided imagery or visualization, it is necessary to focus the attention inward away from everyday thoughts. Concentrating on the breath is one of the most basic techniques for doing this. An easy and effective way is to count your breaths to four with an inhalation and exhalation counted as one. When you reach four, start at one on the next breath and again count to four, repeating this until completely relaxed. Another way is to practice a few deep-breathing exercises in which you exhale and inhale to the count of eight, completely emptying the body of breath, inhaling, expanding the abdomen, the lungs, and filling the body with air. In this initial phase, you begin to relax and direct attention by focused concentration. Instead of using the breath, some techniques use a mantra—a repeated word or phrase—to empty the mind of thoughts.

The next step toward total relaxation involves directing attention to every part of the body from the toes to the scalp. If you must be in a prone position and are apt to fall asleep during these exercises, an arm can be held perpendicular to the prone position supported by resting the elbow on the bed. Should sleep occur, the arm will drop and awaken you. In this totally relaxed state, you are now ready to begin the first visualization, or guided imagery exercise.

PREPARATION

If seated, find a comfortable position in which your posture is erect, your feet are flat on the floor, your arms hang easily from your shoulders, and your hands rest comfortably in your lap. Take a moment to distribute your weight evenly over your buttocks, on your "sitz bones," with your spine straight, each vertebra in line over the one beneath it, comfortably balanced and totally supported. Feel the support beneath your feet, under your thighs.

If in bed, find a comfortable position in which you are completely supported. Feel the support beneath you.

Close your eyes and direct your attention to your breathing.

Begin by exhaling until there is no air left inside.

Take a deep breath, inhaling slowly through the nose, expanding the abdomen and the lungs to their capacity.

Do this three or four times, and as you inhale, repeat to yourself the word *relax.* As you exhale, picture all the stress and tension leaving your body with each breath.

Now direct your attention to the soles of your feet, which are resting on the floor. Beginning with your toes give the verbal message, "Relax."

Continue to direct attention up through the feet and ankles, shins and calves, thighs and buttocks, up through the back to the shoulders. If you notice tension in any part of your body, you may find it helpful to constrict the muscles in that area for a few seconds, then release.

Relax the shoulders and let your arms hang. Continue to relax the arms and fingers.

Direct attention to your neck and scalp, forehead and

face, ears and eyes. You may want to squeeze your face up tight, then release, to help with relaxation.

Focus attention on the jaw, one of the most powerful muscles in the body—and often full of tension. As you relax the jaw let your mouth open comfortably.

Take a few moments to redirect your attention to your breath in this completely relaxed state.

Now you are ready to begin.

Exercise 1—Words in the Cave

Begin to see yourself walking along a path near the sea. Notice how the sun and the soft air feel on your skin; begin to smell the salt air; see the colors of the sea and the sky; put yourself totally in this place.

As you walk, you notice a stairway leading down to the water. Approach the stairs and begin to descend—down, down to the beach. Notice there are rocks along the embankment. In these rocks you begin to see an opening into a cave. You realize this is a perfectly safe place and that within this cave you will find a message written on the cave wall. It is a message meant especially for you.

Begin to enter the cave; feel the coolness of the air; smell its earthy aroma. Notice that the cave opens into a large room with light coming from above. As you look at the wall you notice that some words are written on it. This is the message written in this special place with meaning just for you. Take a moment to read it.

After you have read the message, take a moment to say thank you, to remind yourself that you can return here to this place for a message anytime you like. Turn and begin to retrace your steps back out of the cave, onto the beach, up the stairway to the field overlooking the ocean. Take a moment to look at the beauty you see that surrounds you.

Begin to return to the room in which you are seated or lying. When you are ready, open your eyes slowly.

Exercise 2—Conversation with Your Inner Guide

In your mind's eye begin to see yourself in a beautiful meadow on a lovely day in summer. Take a moment to drink in the sights, smells, colors, and textures of this special place. When you are ready, begin to notice a path leading to the bottom of a hill.

Start to climb along the path that leads up the hill, feeling the coolness of the shade of the huge trees, the smell of the vegetation, the sight of the sun through the trees and its warmth as it falls on your skin. Continue climbing on this path, going higher and higher, until you begin to notice through the clearing that you are high above the meadow. Take a moment to drink in the view before continuing your climb.

You now notice, in a clearing ahead, on the side of the mountain, a beautiful golden cathedral, glistening in the sunlight, with tall fir trees protectively sheltering it on either side. Notice the large open doors into this sacred place, approach them and go inside.

As you enter, take a few moments to adjust your eyes to the darkness within. Notice the sunlight streaming through the windows on golden rays, listen to the quietness, and notice the stillness of this sacred place.

You realize as you sit here in this beautiful and safe golden cathedral that soon your inner guide will join you. Think about the question you want to ask your guide.

You begin to sense another presence here beside you. It is your inner guide come to be with you to answer whatever question you may ask. If you have no question, you may just sit here with your guide and notice and remember whatever feelings, impressions, or sensations you are having as you spend this special time together.

Gently prepare to think about leaving your guide, knowing that you may return to this place or any other place that is special to you any time you choose. Say good-bye to your guide and start to leave the golden cathedral, going back out through the large doors, out into the opening, seeing the path before you that leads back down the mountain, and begin to descend the path. Go down, down the mountain, through the trees until you come to the bottom and to the meadow. Take another look around this lovely meadow and prepare to leave it. Gradually become aware of the room in which you are now sitting. Feel the floor beneath your feet and your sense of body awareness returning. When you are ready, slowly open your eyes.

Exercise 3 — Healing Water

Picture yourself walking along a dirt road in the country on a beautiful day in fall.

Begin to feel the crisp, yet warm, air on your skin, to see the glorious color of the leaves against the bright-blue sky. Take a deep breath and smell the trees, the leaves, and all the rich odors of the earth at this time of year. Listen to the sounds around you.

Take a moment to experience this place with all of your senses. Really be here.

As you enjoy the delights this beautiful day has to give to you, notice ahead of you, on the side of the road, a path leading into the woods.

As you approach the path, notice the beauty of being in the woods on this gorgeous fall day. Notice the contrast of the colors; continue to breathe in the smells and to hear the sounds in the forest as you walk deeper and deeper into the woods.

Ahead of you on the path you begin to see a patch of bright-green color. As you get nearer to it, you see that it is the grass-covered course of a small brook.

As you get still closer, you can see and hear the clear water gently flowing over grasses, stones, and pebbles. Take a moment to enjoy watching and listening to the water as it moves easily on its course. Look downstream and see how easily the water finds its way through the woods.

As you look upstream you become curious about its source and start to walk toward it.

You see a spring of healing water in the ground. Stand above it and look down into its mysterious depths. As you look into the spring, notice the almost imperceptible movement of the surface of the water as it gently, calmly swells up out of the ground and into the stream.

Take a moment to look into the deep source from which the water comes.

Lean down. Scoop some of this healing water into your hands and drink it. As you swallow the water, feel its pure, healing energy moving through your body, healing every part of you as you swallow.

Take one last look into the mysterious depth of the spring, the source, and realize that this source lives within you, feeding you, nourishing you, healing you, and giving you life.

Prepare to leave this special place, the source of healing, and make your way back along the path to the road. As you leave, utter a word of thanks for the gifts you have received this day.

When you are ready, begin to direct your awareness to the room in which you are sitting or lying, and slowly open your eyes.

Exercise 4—Reliving a Favorite Day

Make a list of three or four of your favorite days; days that had special meaning for you; when you felt the best you have ever felt in your life; when your life seemed particularly rich and full. Perhaps you were filled with contentment, maybe excitement. You might have been alone, or you might have been with people especially dear and precious to you. You might have been involved in an activity you really enjoy. Or maybe you were in a favorite place where you felt particularly happy or peaceful.

Take some time and thought to compose this list. It is enjoyable to make a survey of pleasurable memories.

Now that you have some days in mind, you may choose any one of them to relive in your imagination, anytime you need or want to have a pleasant experience, to have relief from pain or boredom, or need to find an inner focus for your thoughts.

Remember to try to recapture the experience with as many of your senses as possible: sight, sound, touch, smell, even taste if that is appropriate. Pay particular attention to the feelings you have as you relive the day in your memory. Realize that you can recapture these feelings whenever you wish or need to.

Property of
Sharon Campbell